SOY & BEESWAX CANDLES MAKING HANDBOOK

HOW TO START A HOMEBASED PROFITABLE CANDLE BUSINESS

By

Rebecca Hall

Copyrighted Material

Copyright © 2017 – **Streets of Dream Press**

All Rights Reserved.

Disclaimer: At the writing of this book, due diligence was done to ensure accurate and up to date information regarding candle making and safety during candle making and starting a home-based candle making business. Information in this book is intended for personal use of the reader only. The information is not intended to replace professional advice for safety or manufacturing or starting a business. The reader reads and utilizes all information in this book at their discretion and assumes full responsibility for the utilization and result of the information. Author and associates, and publisher and associates assume no financial liability or responsibility for any injuries, losses, and/or any other damages that may result from the use of the information in this book.

Published by:

Streets of Dream Press

P.O. Box 966

Semmes, Alabama 36575

Cover & Interior designed

By

Jackie Bretford

First Edition

CONTENTS

Introduction 7
   Soy Candles 9
   Beeswax candles 10

PART ONE 14

Types of Candles 15
   Types of Candles 16
      Votive Candles 16
      Pillar Candles 18
      Molded Candles 19
      Taper Candles 20
      Container Candles 21
      Tea light Candles 21
      Floating Candles 23
      Dipped Candles 23
      Rolled Candles 24
Candle Making Equipment, Supplies, and Raw Materials 26
   Beeswax 27
      Brood wax 27
      Capping wax 28
      Cleaned yellow beeswax 29
      White Beeswax 30
   Where to Find and Buy Beeswax 30
   Soy Wax 35
   Wicking 39
      Wicks for Beeswax Candles 41
      Cored Wicks 42

- Square Wicks 43
- Flat Wicks 43
- Wicks for Soy Candles 47
- Wooden Wicks 49

Scents, Colors, and Additives 51
- Adding Scent 51
- Adding Color 54
- Adding Additives 56
- Where to Purchase Essential Oils, Fragrance, Additives, and Color 56

Candle Making Equipment 59
- Heat Source 60
- Pouring Pot 61
- Double Boiler 62
- Candy Thermometer, Dial Thermometer, or Digital Thermometer 63
- Digital Scale 64
- Molds and Containers 65

Safety in the Candle-Making Workspace 67
- Set Up a Safe Workspace 68
- Safety with Fire and Wax 71
- 7 Additional Must Follow Safety Tips 73
- Safe Cleanup 75
  - Method 1 77
  - Method 2 78

Candle-Making Process and Techniques 80
- 6 Tips for Successfully Using Beeswax 81
- Recipe for Rolled Taper Candles from Beeswax Sheets 82
- Recipe for Beeswax Sheet Ornamental Candles 85

Side Note 88
Recipe for Beeswax Container Candles 89
Recipe for Molded Votive Beeswax Candles 93
Recipe for Beeswax Hand-Dipped Candles 96
Tips for Successfully Using Soy Wax 101
Recipe for Soy Container Candles 101

PART TWO 108
The Business side of the Home-based Candle Business 109
3 Reasons to Start Your Candle Making Business 109
It's Rewarding! 109
Low Start-Up Costs 109
Good Source of Supplemental or Main Income 110
Is It a Business or a Hobby? 112
Legal side of Your Business 117
Business Structure 117
Three Main Types of Business Structures 117
Sole Proprietorship 118
Partnership 119
Corporation 121
Business License, Permits, and Zoning 124
Keeping Records 127
Checking Account and Credit Card 129
Stay Organized 129
Business Cards 130
Domain Name, Website, and Social Media 130
Catalog, Product Descriptions, and Labels 131
Business Plan 133
Inventory Management 136

Inventory 136
Promoting and Selling Your Candles 140
    Selling Online 141
    Social Networking Sites.. 142
    Off Line and Local Sales.. 144
How to Price Your Candles 148
Marketing, Branding, and Promoting Your Candles..................... 152
    4 Effective Marketing Ideas 154
In Review and Conclusion 156
Last words 158
Appendix – Articles of Incorporation.. 159
Appendix –B Business Plan 166
Appendix – C Sample Invoice 172

INTRODUCTION

Whether a beam of safety and assurance when there is a power outage during a storm, the sparkling light on a birthday celebration cake, or the lingering glow of a yuletide flame, candles play a major role in our daily lives. They add warmth, ambiance, scent, and beauty to our homes. When used for holidays, celebrations, weddings, religious ceremonies, romantic dinners, and memorial services, candles are a part of the memories that we cherish.

Candles can also be used for practical purposes such as providing emergency lighting during electricity outages when camping, or if one chooses to live off-grid where electricity isn't available. Citronella or herbed candles keep the mosquitoes away from backyard barbecues, potlucks at the park, and evening dinners on the patio. Scented candles are often used to add scent to a room or to dispel an unpleasant odor such as when cooking fish or in the bathroom.

Scented and shaped candles can become simple or grand center pieces in decorating schemes. Novelty candles are excellent gifts for holidays, birthdays, wedding showers, baby showers, anniversaries, hostess gifts, gifts for office parties, or housewarmings, thank-you gifts, and special occasions.

It is no wonder that the National Candle Association reports that U.S. retail sales of candles are estimated at approximately $3.2 billion dollars per year, and this number does not include the sales of candle accessories (Facts and Figures About Candles, 2017). Candles are highly popular, but today's candle users are discriminating and health-conscious about the type of candles they burn in their homes or give as gifts.

It is now common knowledge that, generally, conventional candles are created from paraffin, which is a petroleum by-product that creates unhealthy air quality when burned. Typically, paraffin candles contain toxic synthetic fragrances and emit fumes that are likened to the fumes of diesel exhaust. Can you imagine diesel exhaust in your living room! Carcinogens and neurotoxins that are linked to allergies, asthma, and lung, skin, and eye irritation are released into the home when paraffin candles are burned.

Fortunately, there are excellent replacements for paraffin candles that don't release toxins into the air of your home: soy candles and beeswax candles. Soy wax and beeswax are healthier alternatives, and both are easy to make at home!

SOY CANDLES

Soy candles are made from hydrogenated soybean oil, which is a natural, renewable source. It's important to note that not all store-bought candles are made from 100 soy wax, and the candle can contain anywhere from a small percentage up to 49 percent paraffin and still be labeled as "pure" soy candles. If you make and sell soy candles, providing the soy percentage on the label can be important marketing information; especially if your candles are 100 percent soy wax.

Soy wax has a lower melting point than paraffin, meaning soy candles usually burn longer than paraffin candles and burn cleaner. This may offset a portion of the higher price of soy candles.

BEESWAX CANDLES

Beeswax candles are, as the name implies, made from natural beeswax. When made from 100 percent beeswax, these candles are often the choice candles for the environmentally conscious and health purists. Beeswax candles burn cleanly, without soot. Beeswax candles can help clean indoor air of bacteria and odors as they emit negative ions when burned. This makes them an excellent candle for burning during winter months when the house is closed to keep out the winter chill.

When beeswax candles are burned, they emit a sweet honey scent that many people prefer to heavily scented candles, but essential oils can be added to beeswax for stronger natural fragrance.

Just as with soy candles, candles labeled as beeswax candles can range from 51 percent beeswax and 49 percent paraffin upward to 100 percent beeswax. Beeswax is more expensive than paraffin, so many manufacturers try to use as much paraffin as possible to offset the cost of making the candle. Offering pure 100-percent-beeswax candles often provides customers with a sought-after treasure!

Candle making is a fascinating but easy process that allows you to make the exact type, style, scent, and color of candle that you want. Candle making can also be a profitable and fun business that provides your customers with delightful unique candles and candles for practical purposes.

In this book my goal is to provide you with all the information you need for making candles and starting a home-based business. In part one of the book, you'll learn what equipment you need, what raw material is necessary for candle making, how to safely make candles, how to add scents and color and shape your candles, and much more.

This book also contains easy to follow recipes to get you started. In part two of this book, you'll learn how to start a home-based business: legal requirements; developing a niche market; packaging and labeling; pricing strategies; promoting and marketing your candle business; where to sell your candles; and how to grow your business. Follow the simple guidance and instructions in this guide and you're on your way to candle-making success!

PART ONE
Candle Making A to Z

TYPES OF CANDLES

Throughout history, dating back to over 5,000 years ago, mankind has used various plant and tree oils, insects, and animal fat to create candles for light. Since the advent of electricity to provide light, candles have mainly been used for emergency lighting, to create ambiance or scent, for décor, or on religious, ceremonial, or celebratory occasions.

Even now, though, on the simplest level, most candles are still molded or dipped wax with an ignitable wick inserted in the wax. In modern history, for many years, candle wax was created from petroleum-based by-products, but with the realization of health and environmental problems from petroleum based candle wax, people often prefer beeswax candles or soy wax candles. Those are the two types of wax this book will refer to during the candle making process.

However, within the category of beeswax or soy wax candles, there are various types of candles. Once you learn the basic types and techniques for making candles, you can experiment, but it's good to know the options for types of candles.

It's inspiring to know that you are not limited to the candles on the shelves of commercial shops. You are the candle artist and can create the masterpiece that pleases you! Think of all the variations of design, shapes, scents, and colors!

However, even the most experienced candle artist needs to start with a plan, and the first step in the plan is knowing the type of candles you want to make. The type of candle will determine what equipment and supplies you need to gather for your candle-making session and how to best set up your candle-making workspace for workflow management.

TYPES OF CANDLES

VOTIVE CANDLES

Votives are poured or molded candles and one of the simplest types of candles to make. They are usually cylindrical or square shaped. Generally, they are about two inches in diameter and two or three inches tall.

They come in this size to fit nicely in standard votive cups. Often, votive candles are used for ceremonies, weddings, memorials, or vigils where people need to hold candles in their hand. Scented votive candles are also used for adding scent to an area.

PILLAR CANDLES

Pillars are also poured or molded candles and among the easier candle to make. Pillar candles are popular as they are long-burning due to their shape and size; are easy to add scent; and come in sizes from around three inches in diameter to very large, multi-wick size. They are usually cylinder-shaped but are sometimes square.

The simplicity of the pillar allows them to be used in almost any décor from elegant opulence to minimalist modern. Often the style of the pillar is determined by the type of candle holder used. Since pillars are heavy and stable, they can stand alone on just about any flat surface or holder.

MOLDED CANDLES

Molded candles are simple to make by pouring melted wax into any type of mold. Molds come in many different shapes and are often made from glass, metal, plaster, silicone, or acrylic for safety reasons, but you can make molds from many containers you may have around the house such as waxed milk and juice cartons, cans, and muffin cups.

TAPER CANDLES

Tapers are dipped candles that are usually at least six inches tall and up to 14 inches tall. The standard diameter for candle holders for tapers is three-quarters of an inch.

Tapers are displayed in candle holders or candelabras as they cannot stand alone. They are often used as statement pieces for romantic candlelit dinners, weddings, or religious ceremonial displays.

CONTAINER CANDLES

Container candles are excellent candles for soy wax since it does not harden as hard as other waxes because the candle remains in the container and is burned in the container after the wax hardens. Today, the more unique the container for the candle, the more attractive the candle.

TEA LIGHT CANDLES

Tea light candles are a practical candle used to create a scent when used in essential oil or scented wax diffusers or under chafing dishes to keep food warm until it is served.

Tea lights are also used in decorative candle holders to shine line through a cutout, such as the "window" of a candle holder designed as a winter cabin. To serve these purposes, tealights are shorter than votive candles.

They may be scented if used in essential oil or scented wax diffusers but are unscented when used to keep food warm.

FLOATING CANDLES

Floating candles are similar to tealights but they are shaped to float in water while burning for displays.

DIPPED CANDLES

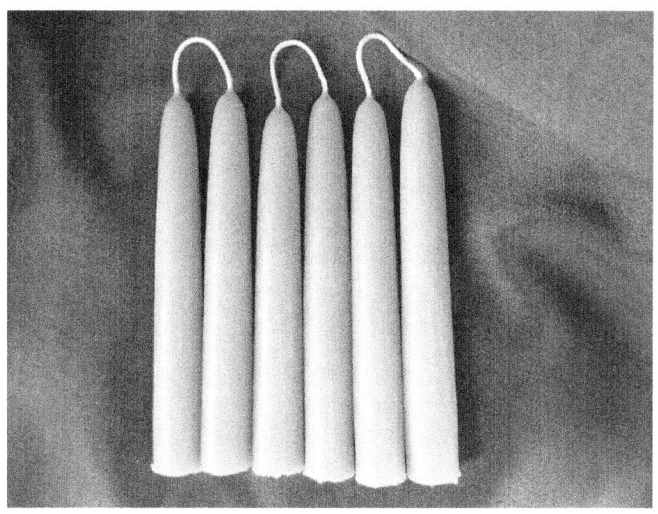

Dipped candles include taper candles and classic birthday cake candles. The candles are formed by dipping the ends of a long wick into melted wax. The wax-coated wick is then hung over a rack until the wax is cooled and then dipped again until the desired candle size is achieved.

ROLLED CANDLES

Rolled candles are super easy to create as they are created by rolling a sheet of beeswax tightly around a wick. The beeswax sheets can be rolled into tapers or pillars of varying diameters. Beeswax sheets are available in dyed colors or the natural golden-yellow color.

You may decide to focus on making one type of candle or several types, depending on your personal candle needs and styles or who your targeted market is for your candle business. But do put some thought into what type of candles you will make before you shop for equipment, tools, and supplies.

CANDLE MAKING EQUIPMENT, SUPPLIES, AND RAW MATERIALS

Candle making equipment and tools can vary, depending on the type of candles you make, but some basic tools and equipment are necessary for making all types of candles. It's best to gather all your equipment ahead of time and organize it. Doing so ensures that you have everything you need for a successful candle-making session.

Having your supplies and equipment available and organized can also make candle making safer. Candle making requires your focus and presence, so it's not safe to leave the work area during the candle-making process to look for supplies or equipment. Lack of organization in the work area can result in accidents or botched batches of candles. You don't want either!

Since candles are all about the wax and wicks, let's start there. As I said before, the goal of this book is to provide information on natural candles, so the focus is on beeswax and soy wax.

BEESWAX

Beeswax candles are clean-burning candles and are in great demand because they emit negative ions that help rid the indoor air of odors and bacteria that create odors.

Beeswax can be purchased in various kinds, and the quality of the wax can vary. It's important that you know which beeswax is right for any specific candle-making project. Here are some types of beeswax that you should know:

BROOD WAX

Brood wax is the lowest quality of beeswax. This is the beeswax that was used in the beehive to house bee larvae. Because the wax is often left in the beehive for several seasons so the bees don't have to create a new honeycomb before they can lay eggs, the wax becomes darkened from the honey and other stuff that is left behind in it. When brood wax is used for making candles or other projects, you must first melt it, adding a little water, so the impurities will sink to the bottom of the melting container and can be strained out. Unfortunately, this process causes much of the wax to be wasted.

CAPPING WAX

Capping wax is a commonly used, golden wax for candles. It is fairly clean but should be rendered, without water, before making candles because it may contain bits of bee parts or honey. Before using, melt the capping wax, and let it sit in the container over a warming candle or other gentle heat source for about an hour while the debris settles at the bottom of the container. Pour the yellow wax on the top into a mold. When it hardens, it's ready to melt for candle-making.

CLEANED YELLOW BEESWAX

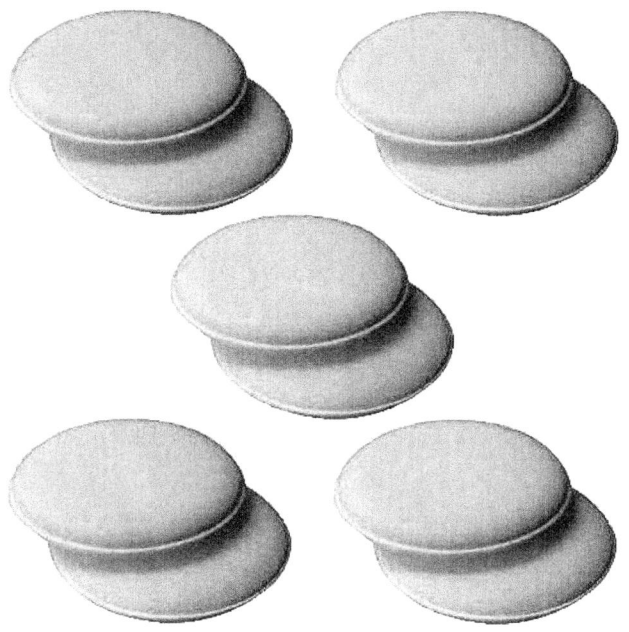

Cleaned yellow beeswax is more expensive than capping wax, but you do not need to render it before using it and, thus, it is usually considered the best type of beeswax for making candles.

WHITE BEESWAX

White beeswax is the purest and most expensive type of beeswax as it contains no debris or honey. White beeswax is pure from filtering through a carbon filter, or it is bleached by UV light treatment.

WHERE TO FIND AND BUY BEESWAX

There are various places where beeswax can be purchased, or you can gather your own beeswax if you should decide to keep bees. If keeping bees isn't your thing, but you want "fresh from the hive" beeswax, check with local beekeepers that might have beeswax for sale. You may be able to locate a beekeeper in your area by visiting the American Beekeeping Federation website: http://www.abfnet.org/ or at *Bee Culture, The Magazine of American Beekeeping* website at http://www.beeculture.com/find-local-beekeeper/ .

CandleWic.com

https://www.candlewic.com/store/category.aspx?q=c20&gclid=Cj0KEQjw2NvLBRCjsq-Qq6TjwecBEiQAF98GMSBGZXDR-V7qdqKGudKdhwQjJwFFBlC_BZuMR5ZiLJcaAuIv8P8HAQ

BulkApothecary.com

http://www.bulkapothecary.com/product/raw-ingredients/waxes-and-butters/beeswax-white-and-yellow/?gclid=CjwKCAjw2NvLBRAjEiwAF98GMQRmxB9ZxJBvtdW2KTKQqa_I42_vJxHm53BAHJjj648R3-MOOgpIBhoCXz8QAvD_BwE

BetterBee.com

https://www.betterbee.com/candle-making/candle-wax.asp

BulkNaturalOils.com

https://bulknaturaloils.com/beeswax-yellow-granules.html?gclid=CjwKCAjw2NvLBRAjEiwAF98GMRvxIZDBZZ5n8fv7PufUyHXfBYpj1ATnN3OY-5u9YLWe52FqFsiIYhoCVbMQAvD_BwE

ThomasNet.com

http://www.thomasnet.com/profile/00567746/frank-b-ross-co.html?what=Beeswax&cov=NA&heading=93020808&searchpos=2&cid=567746

FrankBRoss.com

http://waxes.frankbross.com/viewitems/all-categories/beeswax?

MountainRoseHerbs.com

https://www.mountainroseherbs.com/products/beeswax/profile

CandleChem.com

http://www.candlechem.com/

Beeswax Forms

Commercial beeswax typically comes in sheets, blocks, or pellets. Pellets, sometimes marketed as pastilles or pearls, are very easy to work with because they are easy to measure and they melt quickly.

ire excellent for small, quick, individual but can be expensive and cut into your profit margins if you're using large quantities of wax to make candles to sell.

Thin sheets of beeswax are beautiful and very handy and quick to use, but again, can be more expensive than purchasing a block of wax and melting it for candles. Though more work is required for breaking it down and processing it, blocks of beeswax can be purchased economically in sizes from one-pound blocks to 25-pound blocks or larger.

You can purchase beeswax that is USDA Certified Organic if you want to make sure there are no pesticides in the wax. (Though organic wax is often reserved for making cosmetics, the organic wax may be important to a specific clientele and may be worth the additional cost to provide candles from organic beeswax.)

The price of beeswax varies, depending on where it is purchased, and the quantity purchased. In some cases, the price is less when purchased in bulk. Check prices, and if you plan to continue to order large quantities from a single manufacturer, a a discounted price for repeat bulk orders.

Not all suppliers can honor that type of arrangement, but some may be able to do so and are happy to retain you as a loyal customer. With a thriving candle business, even a five percent or ten percent discount on wax can increase your profit margins.

Some candle makers recommend a wax blend of 75% beeswax to 25% coconut oil. The candle is still natural and the coconut oil added to the beeswax helps prevent the candle from center collapse.

Experiment with this blend and find what works best for your specific customer base.

SOY WAX

Soy wax is a clean-burning, eco-friendly, sustainable wax that is made from the oil of soybeans. Soy bean crops are major crops in the United States in Indiana, Illinois, and Iowa. Once the soybeans are harvested, they go through a process of being cleaned, cracked, and hulled.

Then, they are formed into flakes, and the oil is removed from the flakes. To make the oil solid at room temperature, the oil goes through a hydrogenation process that changes some of the fatty acids in the oil from unsaturated to saturated.

There are various types of soy wax. One-hundred percent soy wax is what most people prefer if they are concerned about burning clean candles with no toxic emissions. Pure soy wax is usually used for container candles as the melting point is lower than a soy-blend wax.

Soy wax is known as a one-pour or single-pour wax, meaning it is soft enough that it won't shrink after it is poured into the container and hardens, and therefore, the wax won't release and leave a gap between the container and the candle. When making pillar candles or tapers, often a soy blend wax is used for the benefit of the candle becoming hard enough to stand on its own without a container.

Some soy candle manufacturers claim that soy candles burn 50% longer than candles of the same size made from paraffin, depending on the environment in which they are burned and how they are stored.

Soy wax is white in color and can be purchased in convenient pellet or flake form. When planning the colors of your candles, it's important to realize that soy wax doesn't accept dye as readily as paraffin, and your candles will be lighter in color than if paraffin is used. For instance, it may be difficult to get a deep red or green for winter holiday candles. One of the beauties of soy candles is the softer, natural colors.

CandleScience.com advertises as "American's #1 soy wax supplier" on their website: https://www.candlescience.com/wax/soy-wax?gclid=Cj0KCQjwnubLBRC_ARIsAASsNNnyQ1ak9FRpXURe-wGKH3MMAK2ameRI0DpE9GVcCSkP1m4dWrQ6lTgaAquUEALw_wcB .

This company also specializes in soy wax for candles: http://www.lonestarcandlesupply.com/candle-making/candle-waxes-and-additives/ .

Candle Chem

http://www.candlechem.com/

WICKING

If you're just starting out with making candles, the wick may be an afterthought. To the new candle makers, the wick is simply a "string" that is inserted for burning the candle.

The experienced candle maker knows the wick is the most important part of the candle. Even if the candle wax is perfect, the candle will not burn properly without the correct wick.

Wicking for candles comes in various sizes and is often made from cotton, paper, zinc, or wood. The correct type and size of the wicking are based on what type of wax is used for the candle, the diameter of the candle, and the environment in which the candle will be burned (drafty, indoor, or outdoor, etc.).

You need a wick that creates a consistent flame size and a well-formed wax pool without dripping down the side of the candle.

The wick needs to be big enough to draw liquid wax into the flame before it drips down the candle, but small enough to melt only a small pool of wax, so the wick doesn't become flooded with too much wax.

WICKS FOR BEESWAX CANDLES

Finding the right wick for beeswax candles can be a little more difficult than for paraffin wax because there are so many variables in beeswax, such as geographic location, when the wax was harvested, and how it was harvested. You can follow the general guidelines for beeswax candle wicks but always be aware of the variables in beeswax when making candles, and adjust if necessary.

Candle wicks include the following types: cored, square, and flat wicks.

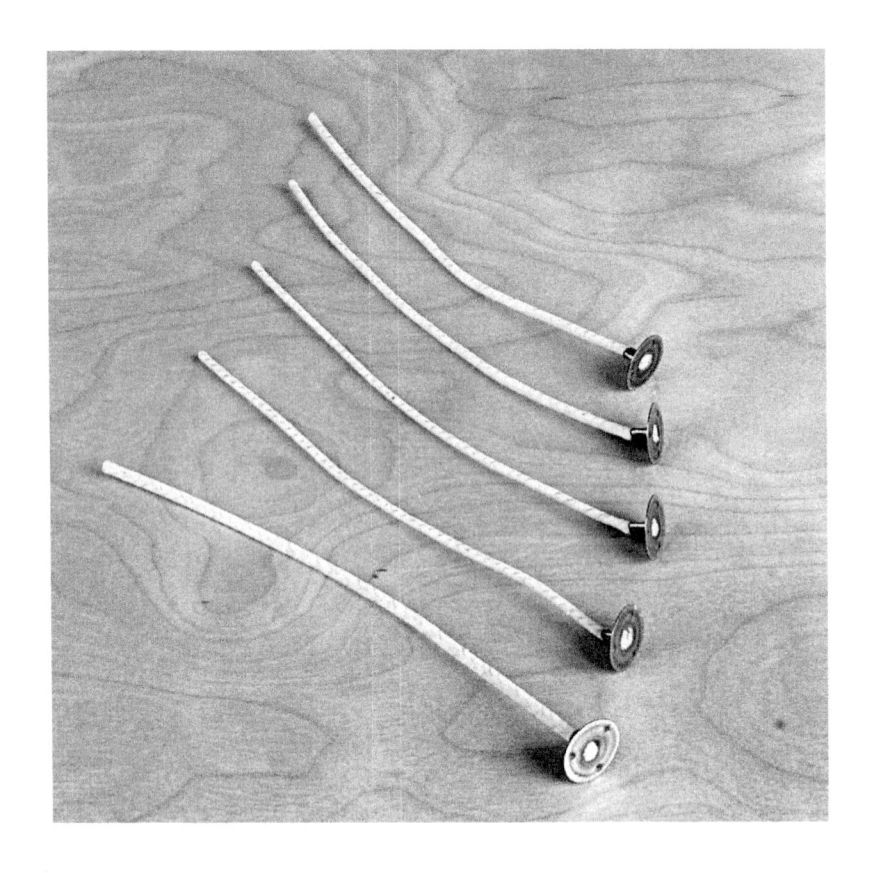

CORED WICKS

Cored wicks have a stiff core made of wire, cotton, or paper. They are often used for votive candles, jar candles, and tea light candles. These wicks are usually purchased already cut to length and with a wick tab attached. The wick tab is the small round or squarish-shaped piece of metal found at the end of the wick to help the wick "stand up" in the container.

Cored wicks burn hotter so the wax can be completely burned.

SQUARE WICKS

Square wicks are the sturdiest type of wicks and are premium wicks for using with beeswax taper and pillar candles.

FLAT WICKS

Flat wicks are braided with three bundles of fiber and are usually used for paraffin candles but clog easily and are not as suitable for beeswax candles.

The size of the wick must be correct for the diameter of the candle. If the wick is too large, it will smoke as the flame will consume the wax too fast. The candle will also flicker if the wick is too large. If the wick is too small, it cannot burn the wax fast enough, and the wax will pool and drip.

To get just the right size wick, start with a recommended size for the wax type and candle diameter, and conduct tests with different wicks in that size range to see if that is the best size for a specific candle. Sample packages of wicks or small packages of each size are sold by many candle-making suppliers so you can experiment without purchasing large packages of one size.

Every variation can change the way the candle burns and what size wick is needed, including how much fragrance or color is added to the wax and the diameter of the candle container. To test wick sizes, make six of the exact same candles, placing a different size wick in each candle. Label each candle container with the wick size (use a dark marker and write in large print on the label) used for that candle.

Line up the candles on a table or counter and make sure the label is clearly visible or tape an additional note to the table in front of each candle. Light the candles. As they burn, every hour, take a digital photo of the group of candles, making sure you capture the top of each candle so you can check the melt pool.

When the candle has burned one hour for each inch of the candle at its widest point, check the melt pool. (As an example, if the candle is three inches in diameter at its widest point, burn the candle for three hours before checking the melt pool.

Be sure to measure the widest part of the candle, not the top of the container that may not be the widest part of the container.) The candle should have a one-half inch melt pool if the wick is the correct size. If the candle has a melt pool smaller than one-half inch, the wick is too small. If the candle has a melt pool that is more than three-fourths inch, the wick is too large.

Candle wick sizing depends on the number of strands of cotton thread in each wick. Wick sizes with the pound sign (#) in front of them are more loosely braided, allowing the wick to expand in diameter. Wick sizes that are "/0" are more tightly braided.

Candle wick sizes increase when the # sign is in front of the number from #0 to #7, but wick sizes decrease from #0 to higher numbers. Use the chart below to determine what size wick you need for making candles with **cleaned yellow beeswax**.

Choosing Your Wick Type

Wick Types	Paraffin	Candle Gel	Soy Wax	Palm Wax	Beeswax	Tealights	Votives	Containers	Pillars
Zinc Core	X	X				X	X	X	
Paper Core	X		X				X	X	
Heinz Coreless	X		X			X	X	X	X
Cotton	X		X	X	X	X	X		X
Wedo RRD	X	X	X	X	X	X	X	X	X
German Coreless LX	X	X	X	X	X	X	X	X	X

Candle Type	Wick Size	Beeswax Weight Per Candle
Tea light	2/0	0.5 oz.
Votive	3/0	2-3 oz.
¾-inch taper	#2	2 oz.
7/8-inch diameter taper	#2	2 oz.
1.5 to 2-in. diameter pillar	#2	3 oz. (can vary by height)
2 to 2.5-in. diameter pillar	#3	8 oz. (can vary by height)
2.5 to 2.8-in.	#4	9 oz. (can vary

diameter pillar		by height)
2.9 to 3.2-in. diameter pillar	#6	12 oz. (can vary by height)
3.3 to 3.5-in. diameter pillar	#7	16 oz. (can vary by height)

WICKS FOR SOY CANDLES

Soy wax burns at a lower temperature than paraffin and blended wax. For that reason, a metal core wick is not necessary for a good burning candle.

Generally, a flat, coreless cotton wick with thin paper filaments interwoven is a good choice for soy container candles. This type of wick, known as the ECO Series Wicks has been designed to be self-trimming to reduce soot and smoke compared to paper-cored wicks.

The Eco Series wicks are coated with vegetable oil instead of paraffin wax so you can assure your candle customers that the candle is all natural if pure soy wax is used. Below is the recommended ECO wick size for typical candle types and sizes.

Eco Wick Size	Candle and Container Size
Eco-1	Small containers and votives 1.25 to 1.5 in. diameter
Eco-2	Small containers and votives 1.5 to 2 in. diameter
Eco-4	Small containers, votives, and pillars 2 to 2.5 in. diameter
Eco-6	Small containers and pillars 2.5 to 2.75 in. diameter

Eco-8	Medium containers and pillars 2.75 to 3 in. diameter
Eco-10	Medium containers and pillars 3 to 3.25 in. diameter
Eco-12	Medium containers and pillars 3.25 to 3.5 in. diameter
Eco-14	Large containers and pillars 3.5 to 3.75 in. diameter

WOODEN WICKS

As customers seek out natural-looking candles, wooden wicks have become quite popular. Some wooden wicks are manufactured in such a way to create a "crackling" sound when burned, like when a fireplace log burns and crackles.

The crackling sound adds to the ambiance of the room.

While wooden wicks are not suitable for beeswax candles, they can be used in soy wax container candles. (Wooden wicks should not be used in votives or pillars.) The recommendation for the wooden wicks size for pure soy candles is the large or extra-large size.

SCENTS, COLORS, AND ADDITIVES

ADDING SCENT

Pure beeswax candles have a wonderful natural honey scent throw, and they naturally clean the air of the room where they are burned. Some customers prefer this natural scent throw and prefer not to have other scents added to the pure candles. Others prefer candles that are lightly infused with pure essential oils.

And there are the customers who prefer a heavy throw from their candles, even if the candle is natural beeswax. Know your customer! This will help you determine what scents to use for your natural candles and how much scent to use.

You can add natural fragrances in the form of pure essential oils or synthetic scents to your candles.

ESSENTIAL OIL GUIDE

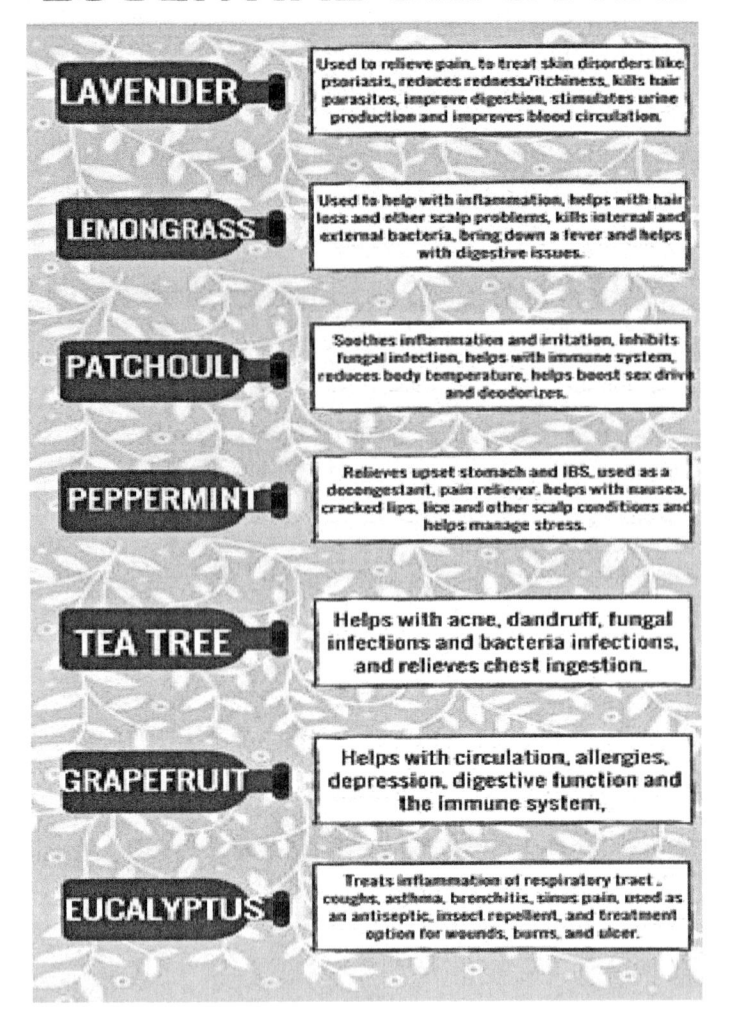

LAVENDER — Used to relieve pain, to treat skin disorders like psoriasis, reduces redness/itchiness, kills hair parasites, improve digestion, stimulates urine production and improves blood circulation.

LEMONGRASS — Used to help with inflammation, helps with hair loss and other scalp problems, kills internal and external bacteria, bring down a fever and helps with digestive issues.

PATCHOULI — Soothes inflammation and irritation, inhibits fungal infection, helps with immune system, reduces body temperature, helps boost sex drive and deodorizes.

PEPPERMINT — Relieves upset stomach and IBS, used as a decongestant, pain reliever, helps with nausea, cracked lips, lice and other scalp conditions and helps manage stress.

TEA TREE — Helps with acne, dandruff, fungal infections and bacteria infections, and relieves chest ingestion.

GRAPEFRUIT — Helps with circulation, allergies, depression, digestive function and the immune system.

EUCALYPTUS — Treats inflammation of respiratory tract, coughs, asthma, bronchitis, sinus pain, used as an antiseptic, insect repellent, and treatment option for wounds, burns, and ulcer.

It's important to keep in mind that using too much fragrance in beeswax can affect the way the candle sets up. Always start with the minimum recommendation in a recipe. In general, use from ½ ounce to 1 ounce of essential oil to 8 ounces of melted beeswax. If the scent is light, you may to add more.

Generally, you can add one ounce of fragrance oil to one pound of soy wax (oil and wax by weight). It's best not to use more than seven percent fragrance by weight, or you may incur problems with wicking.

The formula for adding one ounce of fragrance oil to a pound of wax is as follows: One ounce of oil divided by 16 ounces of wax (one pound of wax) = .625 or 6.25% fragrance load.

ADDING COLOR

Color for candles comes in various forms including liquid candle dye, pigment dyes, and dye blocks. You can use infusions made from herbs and plants to color candles, but you must make the infusion first so that it dissolves in the wax and doesn't clog up the wick. Don't be tempted to melt down old crayons and use the melted wax for coloring as the pigments do not completely dissolve and will clog the wick.

If you want to melt down and reuse old crayons, you can, however, use the wax as a dipping wax for outside layers of tapers or pillars.

Another no-no for coloring candle wax is food dye as it is water-based and does not work for coloring oil-based candle wax. Acrylic paint cannot be used to add color to candle wax.

Dye chips are convenient to use and provide excellent overall color and will produce a lighter color or pastel color with soy wax. Liquid dye also produces a lighter color with soy wax, but the advantage is that liquid dye can be mixed to produce custom colors.

Dye blocks are concentrated color and are an excellent choice for producing darker vibrant colors with soy wax. Keep in mind that wax also appears lighter in color after it has hardened.

ADDING ADDITIVES

Some candle makers also include other additives for better candles. Additives may include the following:

Stearic Acid helps votive candles have a stronger scent, as the votive candles are often used primarily for scenting a room. Add two to three percent stearic acid to the wax.

Modifier helps harden pure soy wax and helps prevent heavy frosting. It also helps create a smoother candle top.

UV Inhibitor is also known as a color stabilizer, and that's exactly what it does!

WHERE TO PURCHASE ESSENTIAL OILS, FRAGRANCE, ADDITIVES, AND COLOR

Pure essential oils can be purchased locally at most health food stores or stores where natural cosmetics and health and beauty aids are sold. Pure essential oils are lovely but can be cost prohibitive unless you are marketing to a customer that requires only the purest, high-quality ingredients in the candle.

If that is the case, the additional cost of pure essential oil is a tradeoff for an elite market. If you serve this market, consider growing, harvesting, and making your own essential oils by infusing oil with the herbs.

Pure, natural, and synthetic scents and colors and other candle-making supplies can be purchased at the following sites, but I do want you to understand one thing,

I am not an affiliate for any of these sites, so I do recommend that you do your own research and find out who offers the best price and quality instead of just relying on these ecommerce sites mentioned here.

Aromatics International

https://www.aromatics.com/products/essential-oils

Mountain Rose Herbs

https://www.mountainroseherbs.com/catalog/aromatherapy

Natures Garden

http://www.naturesgardencandles.com/candle-making-supplies

Glory Bee

https://glorybee.com/aromatherapy/candle-making

Candle Wic

http://www.candlewic.com/candle-making/candle-dyes/candle-dye-colors-pigments/page.aspx?id=1384

One Stop Candle

http://www.onestopcandle.com/CMSU.html

Lone Star

http://www.lonestarcandlesupply.com/candledyes/index.html

http://www.lonestarcandlesupply.com/fragranceoils/index.html

Wellington Fragrance Company

https://www.wellingtonfragrance.com/Fragrance-Oils-C34.aspx?afid=7&trkid=V3ADW128812_2513750152

6_kwd-23341083476_185298118700_g_c_&atrkid=V3AD WA9AD802B_25137501526_kwd-23341083476_185298118700_g_c_1t2&gclid=Cj 0KCQjwh_bLBRDeARIsAH4ZYEMCRZz7yy1W8-JfLLfSOPGEQ7kjLKFY_PKiCRz2HA42a7fMlePKIWcaAu WqEALw_wcB

Candle Making Supplies

https://www.candlemakingsupplies.net/?gclid=CjwK CAjwzYDMBRA1EiwAwCv6JgcC6F2ztYvlGY3-hKq0IN2ZY18QnqKpHMBhS4VzvRSG8YCZxtYgYhoCrx EQAvD_BwE

CANDLE MAKING EQUIPMENT

In addition to wax, wicks, scents, and color, you will need some basic equipment for your candle making sessions. If you're on a budget, start with the basics and add new equipment to your workshop as you can afford to do so. There are several items to make candle making easier and more convenient but are not necessary.

The necessities for candle making are few. Some candle supplies sell basic starter kits that contain the basics such as a melting pot, wicks, color chips or liquid dye, fragrance, thermometer, jars, and labels for a specific number of candles. The kit can be a good way to get started if you want to experiment with a few small batches of candles.

Here is a list of equipment to consider for stocking your candle making workshop:

HEAT SOURCE

Obviously, a heat source is necessary for melting wax. A cook stove with adjustable heating temperatures is ideal for melting wax. However, if you do not have access to a cook stove in your candle making workshop, you can use a hot plate or crock pot for melting wax.

No matter what heat source you use, your first concern when it comes to melting wax is safety—so always keep that in mind when choosing a heat source.

POURING POT

As the name implies, the pouring pot is what is used to melt the wax and pour the melted wax into the molds or containers. For the best results, select a pot that is sturdy with an easy-grip handle and pouring spout. Pouring pots range in size, but a good size is a three-quart size that holds about four pounds of wax.

Most pouring pots are made from aluminum and cost between $9 to around $19. Some candle makers to own a pouring pot for each scent they ently use, so the scent from the previous batch of candles does not transfer to the current batch of wax.

This may be an issue with strong scents but does not seem to be a problem when the melting pot is cleaned thoroughly after each candle making session with lighter scents.

DOUBLE BOILER

It's best not to put the melting/pouring pot directly on the heat source. Use a double boiler to avoid this, but be careful to never splash water into your wax in the melting pot.

CANDY THERMOMETER, DIAL THERMOMETER, OR DIGITAL THERMOMETER

An easy-to-read thermometer helps you monitor the wax temperature to ensure you do not overheat the wax and reach the flash point.

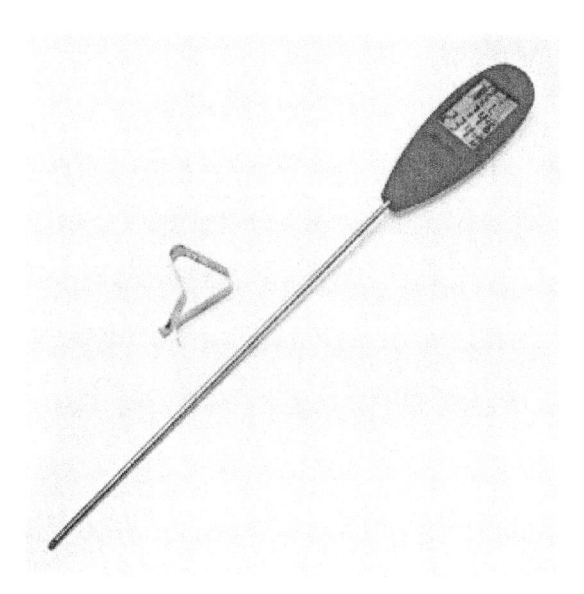

The digital thermometer is the most expensive, but most accurate and easiest to manage.

DIGITAL SCALE

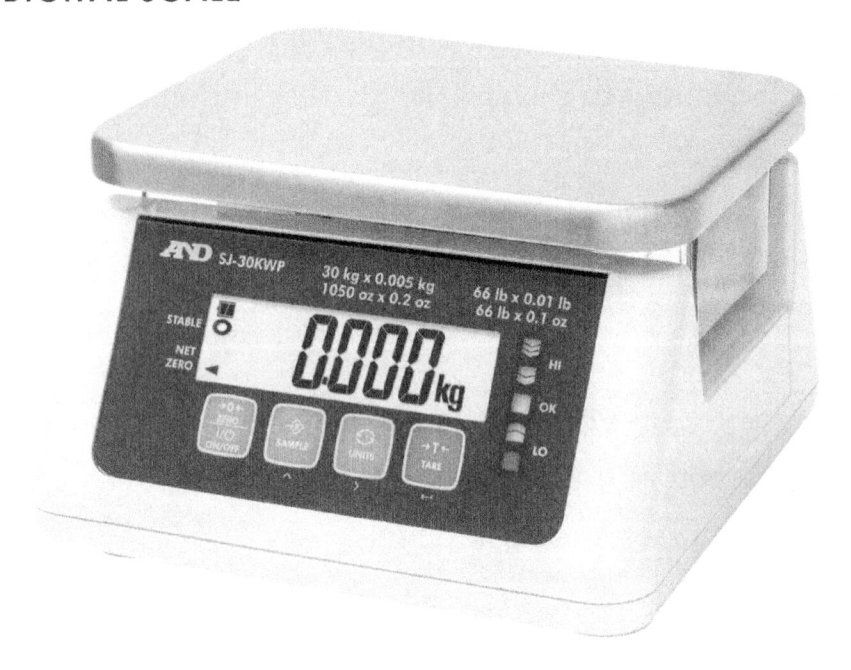

Precision in quantities is important for consistency in the candles. A digital scale allows you to weigh ingredients and record the weight of what you used so you can repeat your successes without guesswork.

A digital scale is quick and easy to read, taking the guesswork out of reading the scale accurately. A digital scale is more expensive than an analog scale, but the difference may be made up in fewer mistakes that contribute to the waste of supplies and time.

MOLDS AND CONTAINERS

Molds come in a variety of shapes and sizes and are made from various materials such as silicone and aluminum. If you enjoy making one-of-a-kind candles, you can create molds out of various household materials such as small waxed juice containers.

The important thing to remember about molds is that you must be able to release the candle from the mold without breaking the candle.

Glass jars of various types are the typical container of choice for container candles when making them in large numbers; however, you can use interesting containers such as small plant pots, tins, small wooden boxes, interesting cups, etc. Be sure whatever container used will not break from the heat of the candle.

SAFETY IN THE CANDLE-MAKING WORKSPACE

Making candles for personal use or for your home-based business can be enjoyable, but it's always important to remember that any time you are working with volatile hot liquid, there is danger involved. You can minimize the danger in the candle-making workspace by taking a few precautions that will help you create a safe working environment.

A candle-making workspace can be set up in almost any space. Many candle makers prefer to work from their kitchen. Some of the most fortunate may have their own candle-making studio so they can store their supplies and leave their equipment set out all the time.

Others may set up a workspace in their garage or in an out building. If you set up in a space that has a reliable heat source and access to water, space for your equipment, and a large, flat surface, you'll be successful in your candle-making endeavors.

SET UP A SAFE WORKSPACE

Candle wax can be messy even in the most controlled environment. It's important that you clear all workspaces of anything that the candle wax could splash on and ruin. You should also cover all counters or surfaces with waxed paper that is securely taped on so it doesn't move around as you work.

Layers of newspapers or other paper should be taped to the floor in the work area. No matter how carefully you work, there are bound to be a few drips, and a few drips of candle wax can ruin surfaces and floors.

For the same reason as you cover all the surfaces and floor in your workspace, when in your workspace, also cover your clothes and your body. Wear clothes that you won't mind ruining if an accident happens. It's best to avoid baggy clothes that can get hung up on equipment and to avoid loose long sleeves that may dip into hot candle wax and burn you.

Wear long sleeves that have elastic cuffs or cuffs that can be buttoned. Wear a flame-proof apron over your clothes. You can purchase these types of heavy duty aprons at candle supply stores or in stores where barbecue grills are sold.

Review your candle recipe or plans and gather all the equipment, tools, and supplies you will need for the entire candle-making session. If molds or other equipment or tools need to be cleaned, do so before you set up shop. Dusty molds will mean dust in your candles. Not good!

Set up the equipment, tools, and supplies in a logical way that allows you to have a workflow without moving things around. Make sure you can reach everything you need without toppling over other supplies or spilling anything.

Always have your recipe or formula written down before you start working. You may know the recipe or formula by heart, but if you get distracted or have a moment where you can't remember, you can quickly ruin a batch of candles. When you are in the process of making candles, you want to think about what you are doing at the moment, not trying to recall a recipe or formula.

You can laminate the recipe or slip it inside a sheet protector, so the paper doesn't get splashed or torn. Try using a cookbook stand to hold your written recipe or tape it to a wall or on the inside of a cabinet door. Another option is to use a clip to hang the recipe where you can easily see it. If your eyesight isn't great, print the recipe in large print, so it is easy to see from a distance.

For the sake of safety, it's best to make candles when you are free of distractions and able to give it your full attention and concentrate on what you are doing. Choose a time when there will not be pets, small children, or other people in your workspace.

Your candle-making workspace should be off limits to toddlers and small children when you are engaged in a candle-making session. No matter how careful you are, accidents can happen and the risk goes up with the distraction of curious toddlers and young children.

Always keep a phone in your workspace so you can call the fire department or medics in the event of a serious accident while you are working. If you wear an apron with a pocket, tuck your cell phone into the pocket, so it's easily accessible for quick emergency calls.

SAFETY WITH FIRE AND WAX

Before you begin working with wax over heat, you must be aware that each type of wax has a *flashpoint.* The flashpoint of wax is the temperature at which the wax will start to burn and flame.

The flashpoint typically varies from between 250 degrees to 400 degrees, but since the flashpoint is different for various types of wax, it's important that you get the flashpoint information directly from the manufacturer of the wax you are using.

It's also critical that you always use a thermometer when melting the wax. You may be able to "eye it" to some extent, but it's risky not to use a thermometer.

If you do not know the flashpoint for the wax you are using, you are at risk for the wax getting too hot and flaming during the melting process.

This can quickly lead to a major fire in your workspace. (There is more information on wax flashpoints, melt points, and pour points in the chapter on making candles.) Always know the flashpoint and never heat the wax beyond the flashpoint!

If your wax does reach the flashpoint and you have a fire on your hands, *do not use water to extinguish the fire.*

Pouring water on the fire will make the flames soar. Instead of water, use a fire extinguisher to put out the fire. If you do not have a fire extinguisher, though it's recommended that you keep one in the workspace, use sand, baking soda, or flour to put out the flames.

Always have a plan of action for the worst-case scenario regarding fire safety while melting and pouring wax. For instance, what would you do if your clothes caught on fire while you are making candles? The best plan is to have several heavy old towels handy for smothering the fire, starting at the point where the flames are closest to your face and moving downward.

This will allow you to breathe. Then drop to the floor and roll to put out the rest of the flames.

What would you do if you spilled hot wax on your skin? Your plan of action should be to have a sink or tub full of cold water and ice cubes on hand so you can submerge your skin in cold water so the wax will harden and can be easily removed before more damage is done to the skin.

If you cannot submerge your skin, at least have cold water available to splash on the skin.

After you have applied cold water to the skin for about ten minutes, you should dry the area and cover it with a sterile bandage and seek professional medical care.

7 ADDITIONAL MUST FOLLOW SAFETY TIPS

1. When you are melting wax, never leave the wax unattended. What could go wrong if you leave the area to chat on the phone, watch your favorite TV program for a few minutes, or go check your email? You never know! And

that's the problem. There are many things that could happen very quickly that could result in a huge fire!

2. When using a double boiler to melt wax, stay aware of the amount of water left in the bottom pan of the double boiler. If the water level gets low, carefully add more water as needed but avoid getting even one drop of water in the wax.

3. Always keep a container of baking soda or sand next to the stove for extinguishing flames that suddenly flare up.

4. Always have a tested and approved fire extinguisher in your workspace.

5. When you transfer wax from the pouring pot to the mold, use a ladle with a long handle to avoid burning your fingers.

6. When you pour wax, do not slosh it out of the pouring container quickly. Pour the wax slowly in a steady stream.
7. Wear shoes when working with hot wax. The shoes should be easy to get off quickly if you spill hot wax on them and sturdy enough for you to retain sure footing without slipping. Obviously, sandals and flip-flops are not a good idea for footwear when making candles, and neither are canvas or cloth shoes that will absorb the hot wax and allow it to burn the skin on your feet.

SAFE CLEANUP

Thoroughly cleaning up after each candle-making session will help preserve your workspace and keep your tools and equipment in the best of shape. Putting away the equipment and supplies without cleaning them first can ruin the equipment or increase the set-up time for your next candle-making session.

You can easily clean your metal tools by putting them in a sink and pouring boiling water over them. Then use tongs to lift them out of the water and allow them to dry on a towel.

Another method is to line a cookie sheet with foil and put each metal utensil on the foil-lined sheet after use. When you're ready to clean up, preheat the oven to 175 degrees, stick the cookie sheet of tools in the oven and let the oven do the work of melting the wax.

Remove the cookie sheet from the oven as soon as the wax is melted, and lift the tools off the cookie sheet with a potholder or tongs. Store the clean utensils and tools in a bin or container, so they are ready for use.

If wax has hardened on surfaces that won't easily scratch, use a plastic scraper or a metal scraper with a rubber edge to gently remove the hardened wax. Don't toss the hardened wax scraps as you can save it to melt and make more candles.

When cleaning up after a candle-making session, don't pour melted wax down the drain. When the wax hardens, it can clog the drain. It's best to pour the melted wax into a container, let it harden, and save it for melting again.

Inevitably, you will accidentally spill or splash wax on fabric when making or burning candles. Candle wax can stain fabric if it remains on the fabric long enough for the oil to soak into the fabric.

That's why it's important to get the wax off as soon as you can. To help the wax harden faster and to keep the oil from spreading over a larger area, put the item the wax is on in the freezer. As soon as the wax hardens, remove it from the fabric. At that point, there are two methods that may help remove wax stains from the fabric:

METHOD 1

>After you have removed the hardened wax from the fabric, place several paper towels on top of each other on an ironing board or surface that is safe to use the iron on. Put the fabric on top of the stack of paper towels, with

the stained area in the center of the paper towel stack. Stack more paper towels on top of the stained area of the fabric.

Set an iron on the low setting with the steam setting off, and press the paper towels on top of the stained area, so the heat melts the remaining wax and the paper towels absorb the wax. Repeat this method a few times until the oily stain is gone, then launder the fabric according to the manufacturer's laundering instructions.

METHOD 2

Here is another method that can be used to remove a wax stain. While the wax is hardening in the freezer, put water in a pan or tea kettle and bring it to a boil. Then pull the fabric area where the wax was located tightly over the bottom of a metal pan or bowl and hold it tightly in place with a rubber band.

Put the pan or bowl with the fabric on it down in the sink. Pour the boiling water from the tea kettle or pan over the spot.

Safety cannot be stressed enough when you are in your workspace. All safety rules should be followed to ensure a smooth work session.

CANDLE-MAKING PROCESS AND TECHNIQUES

Now that you've stocked your candle making work space and you know how to stay safe while making candles, it's time to learn to make the candles that you will use in your home, give as gifts, or market to your customers.

There are various techniques for making candles and many recipes available for various candles, but, in general, it all comes down to having burnable wax and the correct size wick for a candle that burns well. When you first start making candles, it's best to use a tried-and-true formula or recipe.

Once you successfully create a few batches of candles and understand the basic techniques and process, you can start experimenting with shapes, colors, sizes, and scents and expand your candle-making horizon.

6 TIPS FOR SUCCESSFULLY USING BEESWAX

1. Keep in mind that beeswax melts between 140-147 degrees Fahrenheit. The wax can become discolored and the structure damaged if heated to a temperature of over 185 degrees Fahrenheit.

2. The flashpoint for beeswax is 400 degrees Fahrenheit. Never heat beeswax to this point.

3. The best dripping temperature for beeswax is between 155 degrees F. and 165 degrees F.

4. Beeswax that is not hot enough can create pebbly texture on the candle.

5. Beeswax that is too hot will not congeal around the wick.

6. Do not be tempted to take a "shortcut" and melt the beeswax in the microwave. You can't control the temperature, and most microwaves heat at different levels.

RECIPE FOR ROLLED TAPER CANDLES FROM BEESWAX SHEETS

The simplest of all candles may be the rolled taper candles made from beeswax sheets. The candles practically make themselves, yet they are beautiful and practical candles that serve many purposes, including gentle candlelight for the dinner table.

Beeswax sheets come in various sizes and colors from pastels to bold colors. If you want your candles to be completely natural, make sure you check what was used to dye the beeswax sheets as both artificial, and natural dyes are used. One 8.5 x 16-inch beeswax sheet will make two, eight-inch tapers.

To make two, eight-inch tapers, you will need the following supplies:

Supplies

- One 8.5 x 16-inch beeswax sheet (any color)
- Two #2 wicks, 9 inches long
- Scissors
- Hair dryer
- Ruler

Instructions

1. Examine the beeswax sheets. You will notice that each sheet has a pattern that goes in the same direction. When you make the tapers, you want to make sure the grain of the sheet for both tapers is going in the same direction. Think of the sheet of beeswax as a patterned piece of fabric, patterned by cute puppies. If you were going to make a top from the fabric, you would want the pattern on the fabric to be going in the same direction on *both* sleeves, instead of the cute puppies' heads pointing down on one sleeve and up on the other sleeve.
2. Cut the beeswax sheet in half on the long side, so you have two 8.5 X 8-inch rectangles.
3. Working with one of the half-sheets at a time, use the hair dryer to heat the wax just until it

is pliable and can be rolled. Do not use high heat that will melt the wax or heat it for too long.

4. Place the wick along the 8-inch edge of the half-sheet of beeswax. The bottom of the wick will be flush with the end edge of the beeswax sheet. The top of the wick will extend beyond the top edge of the beeswax sheet
5. Firmly fold the edge of the wax sheet over the wick. This step is made easier by using a ruler edge.
6. Roll the wick up into the candle, rolling the beeswax as tightly as you can around the wick. When you roll, try not to crush the hexagonal shapes on the beeswax sheet.
7. Use the hairdryer to gently heat the wax sheet when you get to the end of the unrolled edge. Press the heated edge of the wax sheet against the candle to seal the end seam.

8. Roll the finished candle back and forth with gentle pressure on a hard surface to seal the edge further and make the shape of the candle more uniform.

9. Follow the same instructions to make the second taper.

10. Before burning, let the candles set for a minimum of 48 hours.

RECIPE FOR BEESWAX SHEET ORNAMENTAL CANDLES

These adorable beeswax ornament candles are a fun project for young children and adults alike. They make great gifts and may be a high-demand item for your customers during the holiday season.

One ornament candle can be made from one 8.5 X 16-inch beeswax sheet.

Supplies

- One beeswax sheet for each ornament
- Four inches of size 1/0 wick for each candle
- Cutting mat or several layers of flat cardboard and newspapers
- Cookie cutters in preferred shape
- Hair dryer

Instructions

1. Flatten the beeswax sheet on the cutting mat or layers of newspaper/cardboard. From this

sheet of beeswax, to make one ornament candle, you need to cut out eight shapes that are exactly the same.

2. Place a cookie cutter on the beeswax sheet and press, making sure to create a clean-cut shape. (Don't move the cookie cutter around while pressing!) Cut out another of the same shape until you have eight of the same shapes.

3. Use the hair dryer to warm one of the cut out shapes. Place another cutout on top and press them together firmly. Warm the wax of the second cutout and press the third cutout on top of the first two cutouts. Warm the third cutout and press the fourth on top of the third cutout.

4. Place the wick in the middle of the fourth wax cut out, leaving about a one-half inch of the wick extending beyond the top of the cutout.

5. Place the fifth cutout on top of the wick, taking care to make sure the wick stays in the correct position and is straight, not curved.
6. If the candle has become misshapen as you've added cutouts, now is the time to correct the shape before moving forward.
7. Warm the fifth cut out and press gently to further secure the wick. Place the sixth cutout on top of the fifth cut out. Continue the process until all eight cutouts have been bonded together by the soft wax.
8. Let the decorative candles sit for 48 hours before burning. Before burning, place the decorative candle on a flat candle holder.

SIDE NOTE

You can make Christmas tree ornaments using this process if you replace the candle wick with wicking that is looped and placed between the fifth and sixth cutouts.

The loop allows you to hang the ornaments on the tree. While the ornaments aren't for lighting, the natural beeswax candles will give off a beautiful scent that compliments the pine scent of the Christmas tree.

RECIPE FOR BEESWAX CONTAINER CANDLES

The simple beeswax candle can be dressed up or down, depending on the look you want and style you want to achieve for the candle, and can range from rustic to simply elegant.

You'll be proud of your beeswax candles and can boast that beeswax candles provide a cleaner-burning, longer-lasting candle that not only does not emit toxins into the environment but releases a faint sweet hint of honey when lit. Beeswax candles also clean the air as they burn.

The best wicks for container beeswax candles are cotton square-braided wicks. The correct size wick is determined by the diameter of the container into which you will pour the melted beeswax.

In most cases, if you use a small-mouth jar that measures 2.5 to 2.8 inches in diameter, you will use a #4 wick. If you use a wider jar with a diameter of 2.8 to 3.2 inches, you will use a #6 cotton square braided wick.

In addition to the wicks, you will need the following supplies for making this recipe for beeswax candles

Supplies

- Containers (jars) into which you will pour the candle wax
- Wicking (sizes #4 and #6)
- 12 ounces beeswax, roughly chopped into smaller pieces
- 12 ounces organic palm oil
- Skewers for keeping wicks in place (Pencils can be used)
- Scale for determining weight of ingredients
- Melting/pouring pot
- Wax paper

Instructions

1. Cut wicks for each container. Each wick should be about two to three inches taller than the container.
2. Using the scale, weigh 12 ounces of beeswax in the melting pot.
3. Put the melting pot in a pan of simmering water that is over medium heat, making sure none of the water in the pan splashes into the melting pot.
4. Melt the beeswax slowly. Do not leave the beeswax unattended while it is melting. Stay close by so you can monitor it and not let it get too hot. Wax that gets too hot can ignite!
5. When the beeswax starts melting, dip one of the wicks into the wax to coat it. Carefully place the wick on the sheet of wax paper so that it forms a straight line. You can use the

skewer to manipulate the wick so you don't make a mess or burn your fingers.

6. When the wax dries, tie the end of the wick around a skewer or pencil.
7. Using the scale, weigh the palm oil.
8. When the beeswax is almost melted completely, add the palm oil to the melted wax in a steady stream, stirring carefully as you add it.
9. Immediately pour wax to cover the bottom one-third of the container.
10. Position the wick in the center of the melted wax, placing the skewer or pencil over the top of the jar to hold the wick straight and taut. Make sure the wick is positioned as it should be before you pour the remaining wax.
11. Pour more wax into the container. The wax should be within one-fourth inch of the top of the container.

12. Let the candle cool and harden for, at least, 12 hours, and 24 hours is preferable in most cases.

13. Cut the wick of the candle, leaving about one-fourth to one-half inch of wick above the candle top.

RECIPE FOR MOLDED VOTIVE BEESWAX CANDLES

Molded candles can be very simple or quite intricate, depending on your desired shape and style. Today, molds are typically made from silicone, plastic, or rubber, but tin molds can still be purchased, also.

However, some candlemakers prefer to use antique tin molds for the character qualities. You may also find interesting items around the house that would make nice candle molds. Some candle makers opt to make their own silicone molds or molds fashioned out of other materials.

The thing to remember about molds is that they must be properly prepared for good results. Most molds need to be sprayed with mold release spray before adding the wick and pouring the candle, even though beeswax usually shrinks as it hardens and pulls away from the side of mold naturally. Mold release spray can be purchased at candle-making supply stores.

Supplies for six, three-ounce votives

- 2.5 cups beeswax
- 6 prepared wicks with tabs (stiff center core)
- 6 votive mold cups
- 6 wick pins
- Mold release spray
- Wax melting pot
- Deep pot for double boiler for melting pot

Instructions

1. Spray the wick pins and molds with mold release.
2. Put one wick pin in each mold to mark the center of the mold.

3. Fill the deep pot with water to reach halfway to the top of the melting pot. Place pot over medium heat.
4. Place the beeswax in the melting pot and place the pot in the water, making sure you don't get water in the melting pot.
5. Melt the beeswax over medium heat. Do not leave the melting wax unattended or overheat it.
6. Pour the melted beeswax into the votive molds and set aside to cool. You will notice that as the wax cools, it shrinks away from the wick pin. Pour more wax into the space between the wax and wick pin.
7. Let the wax cool and harden to solid state.
8. Unmold the votives candles.
9. Turn the candle upside down and press on the point of the pin, so the pin slides out of the

candle. You'll have a hole in the center of the candle; this is for the wick.

10. Push the prepared wick from the bottom of the votive through to the top, through the hole created by the wick pin.

11. Trim the wick so that one-half inch remains extended above the candle.

12. Set aside the candles for 48 hours before burning.

RECIPE FOR BEESWAX HAND-DIPPED CANDLES

Beautiful hand-dipped candles are easy to make on days when you have plenty of time on your hands. Though they are a bit time-intensive, the result is worth the effort. Using this method for creating hand-dipped candles, you can make candles of the size of your choice.

Supplies

- Cleaned yellow beeswax
- Wicking that is cut into appropriate lengths
- Covering to protect floor, countertops, and tables from drips
- Wax pot
- Deep pot for melting wax

- Candy thermometer for testing wax temperature
- Rack for drying candles (This can be dowel rods, spring-tension rods, or PVC pipes placed firmly between two sturdy structures (such as doorway), or you can use a wooden drying rack.

Instructions

1. Cover the floor and surface tops of your workspace with a drop cloth or layers of newspaper.
2. Put water in the deep pot so that it reaches about half way to the top of your melting pot. Put on stove over medium heat.
3. Fill the melting pot with cleaned yellow beeswax.
4. Allow the beeswax to melt slowly. Do not become impatient and turn up the heat and risk damaging the wax. Do not leave the room while the beeswax is melting. The melting

could take a few hours so be prepared to do something else in the same work area while the dipping wax is melting.

5. Cut the wicks to two inches longer than the length of the candle you are making. The V of the wick should be upright on the wick.

6. If you are making pairs of tapers and want the tapers the exact same length, tie two wicks in the upright direction at the top. It's not recommended to use one long wick folded over for two candles.

7. When the beeswax begins to melt, prime the wick by dipping it into the wax three or four times so the wax saturates the wick. Straighten the wick so it is not curved at all, by holding the top of the wick and pulling on the bottom of the wick simultaneously.

8. Keep the wick straight when you dip it until enough wax has adhered to the wick to weigh

down the wick and keep it straight. It can be useful to use a skewer or pencil to do this task.

9. Dip the wick into the wax. Hold the wax-coated wick up, but over the melting pot, until the dripping stops. Dip again. Repeat the process until the candle is of the desired diameter. (Note: if you dip the wick several times and do not see a build-up of wax, your wax may be too hot. In this case, lower the temperature of the wax by about five degrees and try again.)

10. Between dips, after the last dip has stopped dripping, roll the candle gently on a hard, cool surface (marble works great!) to help the candle retain a uniform shape.

Here is a YouTube video I found, that explains the process, little differently than how I would do it, but the end result are the same, you will get the idea how it done.

https://www.youtube.com/watch?v=E27yUdPTNEU

TIPS FOR SUCCESSFULLY USING SOY

- Soy wax should be heated to between 150 degrees Fahrenheit to 170 degrees Fahrenheit.
- Soy wax requires more coloring than paraffin wax. Color buttons provide consistent coloring for soy candles.
- Soy wax works great for scented candles. When scenting candles, it's recommended that you don't use more than 3% scent for soy 120 wax or more than 6% scent for S1 wax or PS wax.
- RRD wicks and HTP wicks work well with soy wax.

RECIPE FOR SOY CONTAINER CANDLES

Supplies

- Soy Wax
- Melting/pouring pot
- Thermometer
- Candle jars or containers
- Wick setter—pen shaft or straw to help secure the wick

- Fragrance oil
- Dye
- Sturdy plastic or paper drinking straw
- Paper towels
- Newspapers
- Metal stirring spoon
- Baking sheet
- Pot

Instructions

1. Protect your workspace by covering it with layers of newspaper.
2. Preheat containers to lessen the risk of container breakage and to prevent jump lines. Preheat the oven to 150 degrees Fahrenheit and put the containers on a rimmed baking sheet and "bake" them until you are ready to use them.
3. Measure the wax and place it in the melting pot.

4. Fill the water pot with enough water to reach the halfway mark of the melting pot. Place the pot of water on the stove over medium heat. Place the melting pot filled with wax into the simmering water, careful not to splash any water into the wax.

5. Melt the wax to 150 degrees Fahrenheit to 170 degrees Fahrenheit.

6. When the wax reaches the correct temperature, add the fragrance. Typically, you can add about a ½ ounce to 1 ¾ ounce fragrance per pound of wax used. (For reference, one tablespoon is equal to ½ ounce.)

7. If using dye blocks, cut it into small pieces and add to melting wax. Stir until the dye is completely melted and blended well. If using liquid dye, add a few drops of liquid dye, stir, and add more if needed. It's best to start

sparingly and keep adding the liquid dye as needed rather than add too much that could result in a darker color than you wanted. Although, it's important to note that the liquid wax will appear considerably darker than the wax will appear once it is hardened. You can test a small amount of wax by letting a few drips fall from the spoon onto the newspaper and letting it harden.

8. If desired, add UV stabilizer after you add coloring to the wax. The UV stabilizer helps avoid color fading. Typically, you use about ½ teaspoon of UV stabilizer per pound of wax.

9. When the wax has reached the right temperature, remove the pouring pot from the water pot, using a potholder. Set the pouring pot on a few layers of newspaper before pouring, so the water on the bottom of the

pouring pot will be absorbed and does not drip into your candles when pouring.

10. Take the containers out of the oven.

11. Secure the wicks to the bottoms of the containers. Insert the wick through a straw. Put a dab of hot glue on the bottom of the wick tab, then use the straw to press it to the bottom of the candle container. Pull the straw off the wick and center the wick bar on top of the container. Pull up gently and slide the wick into the slit. Double check to make sure the wick is centered.

12. Slowly and carefully pour the wax up to the widest part of the container, making sure you don't splash the wax and get it on the sides of the container.

13. Let the wax set up. Don't try to accelerate the cooling process by placing the

candle in a cold spot or having a fan blowing over it. Let the wax cool and harden naturally.

14. When the candle has completely cooled and hardened, the top of the candle may look rough or cratered. This is common with soy wax. Leaving the wick bar in place, you may want to pour a second thin layer of wax over the top for a smoother top. Don't remove the wick bar until the last layer is set.

15. Trim the wicks to ¼-inch above the candle surface.

Here is a video of how to make container Soy candles I found on You Tube, take a look, the process again maybe a little different, but the end result is what we desire.

https://www.youtube.com/watch?v=iD_qoAwZrX8

If you're going to market your candles, it's strongly recommended that you put a caution label on the bottom of the candle or the candle container that cautions the user of the candle to follow safety practices when burning the candle and to never leave the burning candle unattended. A caution label may read something like this and can be purchased from candle supply stores, or you can print your own on sticky paper.

> **"Warning!** *To prevent fire and serious injury, burn candle within sight. Keep away from vibrations and drafts. Keep out of reach of children and pets. Never burn the candle on or near anything that can ignite or catch on fire. Always trim wick to ¼ inch before lighting. Keep the candle free of materials such as matches and wick trimmings. Only burn the candle on a level, sturdy, fire-resistant surface. Do not burn the candle for more than four hours at a time."*

PART TWO

Start Your Homebased Candle Business

THE BUSINESS SIDE OF THE HOME-BASED CANDLE BUSINESS

3 REASONS TO START YOUR CANDLE MAKING BUSINESS

IT'S REWARDING!

Starting your own home-based candle business has many advantages. It can be rewarding to work for yourself and invest in your own business over which you have full control.

Besides the pride of business ownership, you can be your own boss, set your own schedule to allow for the things in life that are truly important to you, and work as little or as much as you prefer.

When you own your own business, you can determine your income, whether it be a supplemental income or your main source of income.

LOW START-UP COSTS

With a home-based candle business, you can start with very little money, especially compared to many other home-based businesses. This makes it the ideal business to start right away, not waiting for bank loan approvals, raising capital, or saving for years. The low investment of money also makes it the ideal business for taking a risk.

The worst-case scenario is that you will lose a little money and a little time if you decide this business is not for you.

GOOD SOURCE OF SUPPLEMENTAL OR MAIN INCOME

A candle making business can be a great source of income. The National Candle Association statistics give excellent insight into how many candles are purchased in the US every year, who purchases them, and how they are used.

The National Candle Association website states that candle sales in the United States are at about $3.2 billion per year (Facts and Figures About Candles, 2017). The same report states that seven out of ten households use candles, and most candles are purchased by women.

Unless only used for decorations, candles are disposable, meaning they need to be replaced when used. Consumers use the candles they purchase within one week of the purchase, according to the same report mentioned above.

There is always a market for candles as they are used for lighting, adding scent to a home or workplace, gifts, religious services, celebrations, and decorative focal points.

The fact that customers can purchase home-made candles from local artisans creates, even more, sales appeal. People enjoy supporting the arts and crafts movement and feel good about spending their money at craft fairs, church bazaars, and farmers markets.

During these times of economic uncertainty and job layoffs, having a source of income that you have control over can help you feel more secure about your future financial picture.

Financial advisors agree that having more than one stream of income is a smart strategy against economic turmoil.

IS IT A BUSINESS OR A HOBBY?

A home-based candle business is quick and easy to start as far as businesses go. However, there are still a few legal issues that must be addressed. In this chapter, you will learn what you need to do to make your candle business a real business versus just a hobby.

There is nothing wrong with having candle-making as a hobby. Many people are passionate about making beautiful candles but are not interested in running a business. If you want to have a candle business, you must be interested in starting and operating a business.

If you want to create revenue and make a profit, you must look at your candle business as a business and not as a hobby.

People who start and operate small businesses successfully know they must take their business seriously. This means they must have a plan, albeit, the plan for a candle business can be simple.

They must have a way to fund the business whether through using savings, putting the start-up costs on a credit card, or taking out a small loan.

If you want to successfully operate a candle business, you must have a marketing plan. A marketing plan is the backbone of a successful business. After all, what good will it do for you to work hard to build up your candle inventory if you do not have any customers to purchase the candles and create the income you desire?

Prospective customers must know about your business before they can purchase your candles!

Even though you are your own boss when you own a candle business, any successful business requires the business owner to use self-discipline to show up and do the work required for the business to be successful. This means you must constantly improve your candle-making craft so that you turn out great candles consistently.

It may mean that you must learn how to "sell" because you are naturally an introvert. You may need to study how to best display your beautiful candles, so they are more appealing to prospective customers.

Maybe you don't understand good bookkeeping principles, and you need to take a course at the community college in order to keep from getting in trouble with the IRS? Whatever it is that you need to learn and do—you must be willing to do so for the sake of a successful candle business.

No business can run itself! Sure, you can let someone else run your business for you, but the most successful candle business will require your talents, decision-making, and effort.

If you're not willing to invest in your candle business, you may become disconnected from the business and won't realize the reward of achievement as your business expands and prospers.

How much time can you devote to a candle business? Be realistic. Can you spend 30 hours per week making and marketing candles? Are you still working another job that would limit you to making candles one day per week and taking them to market on Saturdays?

It's important to be realistic about the time you can devote to your business. This is best decided before you start the business, so time to work isn't an obstacle that makes you regret starting a candle business.

Make up your mind now that you will give your business the time and attention it deserves for a fair chance to compete in the marketplace and create a source of revenue for you. This may mean giving up some personal time or recreational time. It may mean changing some of your priorities or giving up some hobbies.

Determine whether you will have help with your business. Do you have a spouse or family members that can occasionally help (with pay, of course)? Can you hire responsible local teens or college students to help as needed or on a part-time basis?

One person can operate a candle business, but what happens if you get sick or need to be away for a few weeks for a family emergency? Is there someone dependable to step into your shoes and fill the gap until you can get back to the business?

Do you have resources for packaging of the candles? For shipping the candles? Do you have markets in mind for selling the candles?

There are many considerations as you get started in your candle business, but don't worry. There are simple solutions and answers, and you'll learn many of them in this unit about starting your candle business.

LEGAL SIDE OF YOUR BUSINESS

BUSINESS STRUCTURE

Even though you will be the owner of your candle business, the government will require that you pay taxes on the revenue that your business creates. For that reason, the government requires that you decide what form of business entity you will establish so that it can determine how much income tax you will pay and what form you will use to file your taxes each year.

Some small business owners make the mistake of skipping this first step and later regret it when they must pay taxes!

THREE MAIN TYPES OF BUSINESS STRUCTURES

Let's start off this book by getting down to brass tacks. The very first thing you should do after you have conceptualized your business is to do choose a structure that will facilitate its operation.

Basically, there are three types of small business structures that you can adopt -

1. Sole Proprietorship
2. Partnership
3. Corporation

Read on a bit further to help you decide which business structure format best suits your business situation.

SOLE PROPRIETORSHIP

A sole proprietorship is the simplest, most autonomous and least expensive way to start a business. That's because "the buck stops with you." You are your own boss.

Expect to pay a fee to obtain a business name registration, a fictitious name certificate and any necessary professional licenses. You can also expect also to pay an attorney to prepare the documents required to legitimize your business.

As you are the only owner, you also retain complete control over the business and are 100% accountable for its failure or success.

PARTNERSHIP

If you are going into partnership with someone else, it is highly recommended that you get a lawyer to administer the agreement. That is because there are several different types of partnerships that can exist. For instance, being in partnership with a franchise is a lot different than being in partnership with an unnamed investor, which in turn is a lot different than being in a 50-50 partnership with your buddy from college who has agreed to launch the business with you.

Each business situation that requires a partnership is clearly unique on to itself, and you really do need a lawyer to draw up any necessary legal agreements.

Still, even though several types of partnerships exist, they are subcategories of the two most common types -

1. General partnerships

2. Limited partnerships.

A general partnership can be formed simply by making "an oral agreement" between two or more persons. However, this is not the way to go if you want to avoid problems down the line if the two of you disagree, have a dispute or decide to go your separate way! This is because this type of agreement is based on each other's "word."

The rule of thumb is that whenever you are involved with anybody else in business, you should make sure to leave a "paper trail."

A legal partnership agreement drawn up by an attorney outlines he division of responsibilities, profits and other joint matters of the business...

Are there any drawbacks to a partnership? If your partner is corrupt, you could be liable for his or her action. The plain fact is that partners are responsible for each other's business actions, as well as their own.

You can also get do-it-yourself legal agreements online to form a partnership. However, regardless of which way you decide to go with this a Partnership Agreement should include the following essential information -

- A description of the type of business

- The mission statement of the business
- Amount of equity expected to be invested into the business by each partner.
- A description of the division of profit or loss
- A detailed description of the compensation that will be due to each partner at certain milestone events or dates
- A description of who gets what assets on the dissolution of the business
- An agreement regarding the duration of the partnership
- Provisions for changes to or dissolving the partnership.'
- A dispute settlement clause
- Restrictions regarding authority and expenditures
- A description of which partner gets what in the case of death or an illness that prevents the running of the business

CORPORATION

A corporation is usually the most complex and more expensive to form than the other two business structures. Control of the business depends on who owns the most stock in the company. The running of the business is exercised through the regular board of directors' meetings and annual stockholders' meetings.

Records must be kept to document decisions made by the board of directors. Small, closely held corporations can operate more informally, but keeping excellent records is a requirement of running this kind of business as there are usually a lot of different variables that govern how it will be run.

Although many small business owners will incorporate for tax purposes or to protect their personal assets in the case of bankruptcy, this is not the same as a corporation which is usually reserved for larger business entities. If you do decide to incorporate you should consult a business attorney so that it is done properly.

Becoming a corporation is expensive, unwieldy and can take a long time to create. If you are an entrepreneur, you probably want to stick to simpler business entities such as the sole proprietorship or a partnership.

You can find more information on how to structure your candle business at www.irs.gov.

However, in many cases, a small, one-person business starts out as a sole proprietorship because it is the simplest business structure. A sole proprietorship is a business that legally has no separate existence from its owner.

In other words, YOU are the business, and YOU are responsible for all the income, debts, and taxes of the business as if they were solely your own personal income, debt, and taxes owed. If someone sues your business—you are the one being sued. If you get a million-dollar account for candles, you get the million dollars.

So, you can see that you are held responsible for all dealings with your business if you are structured as a sole proprietorship.

Sole proprietorships are easy to form, and that's one of the main reasons you may want to start with that structure.

Forming an LLC or corporation can be time intensive and expensive and delay the start of your business.

Another benefit is that, with a sole proprietorship, you do not have to pay unemployment tax on yourself.

BUSINESS LICENSE, PERMITS, AND ZONING

EIN or Employer Identification number is essentially a social security or tax identification number but for your business. IRS and many other governmental agencies can identify your business via this unique 9 digit number.

Remember you will not need this number if you choose to be a sole proprietorship for your business.

It is simple to apply, either you can do it yourself or get your accountant to apply for you, but the process is simple, you fill out the form SS-4, which can be filed online, via Fax or via mail.

Here is a link to IRS website where you can download or fill out the form online.

https://www.irs.gov/businesses/small-businesses-self-employed/how-to-apply-for-an-ein

Some businesses require a federal license to operate the business, but a candle business only requires state or city licensing, depending on where you live. Your candle business may also require permits from the city or county. The permit to operate the business from your home may be partially dependent on the zoning restrictions for where your house is located.

The process for getting a state or city license to operate your business is not costly or complicating. In most cases, it's a matter of filling out forms and paying the license or permit fee. If you're set on starting your business, don't let this bit of paperwork and small fee deter you. It's just part of doing business!

Before you open your candle business, check your homeowners' insurance policy, and read the fine print. Some insurance policies will not cover home claims if a business is being run from the home. Also, check with your homeowners' association to make sure home businesses are allowed.

In some cases, home-based businesses are allowed if there is no customer traffic at your home and with other stipulations that could protect the privacy and order of neighbors.

In other cases, there are no home-based businesses allowed. The same goes if you rent your home—check with your landlord or management company regarding the legalities of a home-based candle business.

KEEPING RECORDS

Once you have established that you can have a home-based business in your home and have secured your business license and permits, set up your record keeping system NOW. Don't be tempted to put this off, thinking you'll get to it later. Later may never come, but the need for records for filing taxes will definitely come, and sooner than you think!

Setting up basic business records for a sole proprietorship can be very simple. You can set up records with a program such as QuickBooks or other software or simply use paper ledgers.

If you are too disorganized to handle record keeping for your business, consider outsourcing that task and have a bookkeeper meet with you weekly to record the necessary information. However, this will still require you to keep track of expenses and income.

Basically, you need to keep the following records and information:

- Expenses
- Income
- Money spent on materials and supplies
- Cost of making each unit
- Units sold
- Revenue from units sold
- Any marketing, Free or BOGO promotion cost

You must have a system to bill your customer accounts if you're selling candles to other businesses. The usual system for this is to send or give the business an invoice with the amount they owe, what they owe the amount for, the date the invoice is due, how to submit payment, and your contact information. There are many templates online for invoices.

You should have receipts available for individuals who purchase your candles at farmer's markets, trade shows, etc. with a tear-away portion for you to keep so you can keep track of the day's sales.

CHECKING ACCOUNT AND CREDIT CARD

Open a separate checking account and have a separate debit card for your business. Doing so will help you keep better records and prevent you from constantly spending "company" money for personal items and bills.

If feasible, set aside a specific credit card for business use. You never want to get stuck without the means to buy more materials if you get a large order.

STAY ORGANIZED

You should keep a calendar (paper or on your computer or device) that helps you keep track of the market dates where you'll sell your candles, sales meetings with store owners and businesses where you want to sell your candles, etc.

You should keep a schedule that outlines when you will make candles and how many units you will be shipping or displaying for the market.

Keep a list of businesses/individuals you want to contact for sales.

BUSINESS CARDS

Paper business cards are not yet obsolete and can be highly beneficial for the small business owner. Order some professional looking cards that are simple but provide your name, phone number, email address, and website URL. Inexpensive business cards can be purchased at www.vistaprint.com.

DOMAIN NAME, WEBSITE, AND SOCIAL MEDIA

Choose a domain name that is easy for people to remember and one that represents your business well. Prospective customers should be able to know what your business is by your domain name. Avoid having hyphens and odd punctuation in your domain name. Keep it as simple and easy to remember as possible.

Even if you're not tech savvy, creating a simple, professional website is not difficult with all the templates available now. Another option is to hire a high school student or college student to create the website for you.

It's okay if your website is simple, but the copy on the website should be well written, concize, and meaningful. Too often, websites contain way too many words but say very little. Adding appropriate pictures makes a website more interesting.

Social media accounts such as Facebook, Instagram, and Twitter can be useful for letting others know about your business. Just remember to keep your posts, pictures, and tweets professional! Your business social media pages represent your business! The pages should appeal to the type of customers you want to attract.

CATALOG, PRODUCT DESCRIPTIONS, AND LABELS

Depending on who your customers are, you may benefit from a professional looking catalog that contains pictures and product descriptions of your best-selling candles.

A good picture and product description is a powerful marketing tool! Take excellent, high-quality photos of your best candles for your catalog. If you don't feel you can write good product descriptions, hire a writer to write the descriptions and labels for you.

One of the cheapest way to get product description, labels, logo, and business card design even some social media marketing is by going to Fiverr.com.

On this site, you will find designers, marketers, writers and pretty much everything else your business may need for $5 each. It is one amazing site, and you can get some much done for so little.

BUSINESS PLAN

If you need to secure funding for buying equipment and supplies for your candle business so you can start with a substantial inventory, you may consider applying for a small business loan to launch your business.

If you apply for a loan to start your business the bank or financial institution may require you to present a business plan that defines your business and how you will operate it and shows that your business is viable and capable of creating an income that will allow you to pay back the money you are borrowing.

A professional, persuasive business plan is sometimes the difference between having a loan approved or denied. There are many excellent books on the topic of writing a business plan.

You can write the plan yourself or hire a copywriter to write the proposal. If you write the proposal, follow the correct format, and include the necessary components.

If you are on a tight budget, you can look on Fiverr.com to find someone to help you with your business plan. You can also go to more traditional sites like Guru.com or Upwork.com where you can post an ad and hire a professional to write your business plan, but that will cost you more than what you can get done on Fiverr.

Then again you get what you pay for; the quality will obviously be much better if you hire a true professional from one of these freelancer sites.

In addition to presenting your business plan to lenders, the plan can be helpful for you. It can help you remember your business goals and help you stay on track. A business plan is highly recommended, no matter how small your business is.

I am attaching a sample Business plan at the end of the book, feel free to use it, copy it or get ideas from it.

If you need a copy of this Business plan in Word format, feel free to email me at rolpublishing@gmail.com I will email you a copy.

Now that some of the basics of launching a business have been covered let's look at some of the main aspects of operating your candle business!

INVENTORY MANAGEMENT

You know that unless you create and sell candles, you won't make any money. Making money is the reason you are in business! Let's discuss what you'll make, how you'll price your candles, and how and where you'll sell the candles.

INVENTORY

Obviously, before you can sell candles, you must choose the candles you want to make and make them. The candles you make and have on hand is your inventory.

If you want to consistently sell your candles for a steady flow of income, you must replenish your inventory faster than you sell your candles. Planning and monitoring your inventory ensures that you always have candles on hand to sell. This is important. Let's use Carrie as an example of why inventory stock is important:

> Carrie created the inventory that she thought she'd need to sell candles at her first farmer's

market. She took 50 candles to the market. By the end of the day, Carrie only had two candles left unsold. She was ecstatic that she had done so well at the market.

The day after the market, Carrie realized she only had two candles left to sell. Her inventory was very low, meaning she needed to make candles before the next farmer's market that she was scheduled to attend in just five days.

However, Carrie blew off making more candles and spent the afternoon shopping. The following day, Carrie again ignored the nagging feeling that she had no inventory. She shushed the nagging worry by telling herself that she'd make candles the next day and still be ready for the farmer's market in time and spent the day cleaning out the garage instead of making candles.

The following morning, Carrie received a phone call from a shop owner who had purchased a candle from Carrie at the farmer's market a few days before. The woman said she was having a special event at her shop and the candles would be perfect for the event.

She wanted to order 40 candles for the event and said if all went well, she would order an additional 40 candles each week. As Carrie added up the dollar amount she would receive for 40 candles each week, she became excited. Then the woman on the phone said, "But I need them delivered by the end of today to use them in the shop tomorrow."

Carrie's excitement turned to disappointment. She knew there was no way she could restock her inventory so quickly and fill the order.

Carrie learned her lesson to always take advantage of the time when it was available to restock inventory in case a surprise order came in. While Carrie knew she couldn't keep a huge inventory on hand, she realized she needed to keep a *reasonable* inventory on hand. Knowing this prompted her to set up her schedule accordingly with specific market days and specific candle making days.

At first, when considering your inventory, you may be undecided about how much of any one candle you should make. You will easily solve this problem as you gain a better understanding of your target customers and if you monitor your sales carefully and determine which candles are selling best in which market.

PROMOTING AND SELLING YOUR CANDLES

In your candle business, you can sell candles to individuals (retail—where you sell directly to the customer) or sell to other businesses (wholesale—where the business sells your candles to the customer) or to both. Whether you sell retail or wholesale or both will determine where you sell your candles and how you sell them.

There are advantages and disadvantages to selling directly to the customer. If you are a natural salesperson and enjoy being around other people, retail can be enjoyable.

You may already be very good at sales, or you may need to learn how to sell your candles. You can learn how to sell products by reading books, articles, and blogs on the topic. You can also attend business organizations that offer tips and help on business topics such as sales.

If you're an introvert and don't like talking to strangers, let alone trying to sell them something, retail may be a problem for you if you don't desire to learn to sell. In that case, consider hiring a sales person.

If you sell directly to your customers, you get to keep the full price of the candle. If you sell to other businesses, they keep a percentage of the price of the candle. This may mean you need to mark up your candles more than you're comfortable with.

It may also mean selling fewer candles. However, if your candles are sold to a business that sells a large number of the candles consistently, you may come out way ahead money wise, not to mention that you don't have to sell face-to-face to customers if you don't like selling.

SELLING ONLINE

If you sell directly to customers, you must have a place to sell your candles. Your online shop could be a website from which you sell the candles, or it could be a situation such as Etsy.com, Amazon.com, or EBay.com.

One of the best ways you can setup an online store is by going to Wix.com; this site helps you create an online store in just a few hours even if you have no idea how to design or setup a store. They even offer all types of payment options for your customers, so in just a day you can have a full blown online candle store for under $100 a month.

To attract and bring new customers you may have to spend some money at first. One of the best ways to attract online customers is PPC (Pay per Click) advertising.

This type of advertisings are done through Google and few other search engines, but my advice would be to stay just with Google. You can also consider running Facebook ads.

The cost are pretty similar to running Google ads, but sometimes you may see better results with Facebook than Google ads.

SOCIAL NETWORKING SITES

This is by far the best way to market your products. Before you build websites or even a domain name, you should focus on marketing on sites like Facebook.

For me, Facebook provided the best results, and I believe it can do the same for you too. If you are like and don't know how social media marketing works, then hire someone from one of those sites I mentioned and let them help you.

Once you see some success, then you should want to invest and get a website ready where you can display all your products and have shopping carts installed so people can buy directly from your site.

Customers want a way to contact sellers directly as well as a place where they can publicly express their shopping experiences.

If you provide this, you will not only draw attention to your business, but you can also potentially increase sales. Keep in contact with your customers through networking sites such as Facebook and Twitter.

Just remember to always include a link back to your website so people can find you easily.

OFF LINE AND LOCAL SALES

Your candle shop could also be set up at one of the following:

- Farmer's Market
- Craft Bazaar
- Holiday Bazaar
- Festivals
- Art Shows

You can also present your candles for fund raising for local school band programs, sports programs, and music programs. Other fund-raising organizations may include churches, youth groups, parks and recreation groups, PTA groups, etc. Just approach the head of the organization and offer them a prepared proposal for buying your candles at a regular price or a slightly reduced price and selling them for a higher price so they can keep the difference for their organization.

Not only does this bring in mega sales for you, but also establishes you as a business person who is active in your local organizations. The publicity can be excellent for your small candle business and help the business achieve growth.

You can also sell candles directly to customers using the party plan. Think Tupperware! Find friends to invite their friends over for a fun evening while you demonstrate and sell candles at the party.

Give special rewards to the friends who are willing to sign up to host a party of their own.

Florists, wedding planners, event planners, gift shops, bath product stores, natural food and product stores, interior designers, and home stagers for realtors are businesses that you should approach with your candles if you're interested in selling to other businesses.

When selling to other businesses, keep in mind that labeling and packaging will be important and should be appropriate for the business to which you sell.

Don't be afraid to approach friends, family, friends of friends, and acquaintances if you feel they would have a need or use for candles. For example, if your daughter's teacher is getting married, ask if you might show her your wedding candles and see if she would like to place an order.

Chances are, she will order, and she will also tell the other teachers where she ordered the candles. The next thing you know, you'll be getting orders for candles from several people in your community for weddings, piano recitals, church services, anniversary parties, and other special occasions.

Always keep in mind that there will be heavy sales seasons and quieter sales seasons. The winter holidays are a big season for candle sales as is Valentine's Day. Don't wait until a few weeks before the big sales seasons to start making seasonal candles.

Shoppers start shopping for holidays early. Stock seasonal inventory for fall, winter holidays, and Valentine's Day ahead of time so you are ready when the season hits!

If you conduct yourself as a professional business owner, consistently produce quality products, deliver on time, and offer excellent customer service, word will get around about your candles and your professional business practices.

Your business will take off faster than you dreamed possible! You will constantly be finding new avenues for promoting and selling your candles.

HOW TO PRICE YOUR CANDLES

To calculate your price point, do your research and find out what similar candles are selling for in the market. Make sure you compare apples to apples and oranges to oranges when you compare your candles to others on the market.

Also, ask friends and family members what they would pay for this type or that type of candle. If possible, try to get people to fill out questionnaires about what they would pay for certain candles. You can also test the market by changing prices on your candles to see how customers respond.

You may find that when you set up shop in artsy areas, the customers don't blink at paying $25 for a small candle but when you set up at the neighborhood farmer's market, people expect to pay less for the same candle.

To come up with an effective pricing strategy for your candles, it is always a good idea to gather information on your competitors. Find out what their market share is, what their marketing strategies are, and what their sales channels and pricing strategy is.

Here is a simple way you can do a competitive analysis. On a piece of paper write down the following:

1. Number of local competitors you have
2. What is their niche/what type of candles they sell
3. Where they sell
4. What is their pricing

Once you have that list, take a look and see where you would fit in that list, how can you stand out from the crowd, what can you do differently that would make customers pay attention to your products.

There are three ways you can always stand above the crowd. I always have tried to stand above the crowd by trying of these three strategies.

1. By making superior products than my competitors make
2. By offering 100% customer satisfaction guarantee
3. By creative pricing strategy

Many customers balk at paying shipping rates, which seem to be quite high now. If you can find a way to offer "free" shipping or a lower flat-rate shipping, it may help with candle sales online.

When you figure out what the market will bring for any given candle that you create, calculate what it costs you to make the candle. Include materials, labor, packaging, shipping if shipped, and delivery, etc.

The difference between what it costs you to make the candle and deliver it to the customer or business and the amount the customer pays for the candle is what you make per candle. If you're paying attention to the numbers, you will be okay!

Pricing is the most important factor of your business. A carefully thought out pricing strategy can make you very successful but a pricing strategy that places you above your market can literality put you out of business and on the other hand pricing below the market can wipe your bottom line profit completely clean, and before you know it, you are out of business and in debt.

That was the risky part; now the tricky part is if you stay with the market, then you are standing out in the crowd instead you are standing in the crowd.

To make yourself more visible and unique and to stand tall among other competitors, you have to be really very creative when it comes to your pricing strategy, and that is where the tricky part comes is.

My goal is to teach you how to implement a carefully thought out pricing strategy that can make you stand out and make you successful.

MARKETING, BRANDING, AND PROMOTING YOUR CANDLES

Most candles are similar in appearance. They come in standard colors, shapes, and sizes. If you go to any store where candles are sold, you will see basically the same candles as in the next store. One of the great things about making your candles by hand is that you can design unique candles.

You must decide who you want your candles to appeal to. You may say, "I want my candles to appeal to everyone!"

That would be nice, but that is not how marketing works. You need to design candles with a specific customer in mind. You need to ask yourself what would make a certain demographic buy your candle. What shape and scent of candle does this age group buy? What type of candle do men buy?

Will you sell sparkly candles to teenage girls? Will you sell party candles? Will you sell elegant, romantic candles?

Will you sell candles that are natural and rustic looking that might appeal to the outdoorsy, natural, healthy customer?

Keep up with industry news about candles. Study the market trends for candles. This is how you can determine what type of candles are selling to what demographic. Read reports such as this one: http://www.businesswire.com/news/home/20170811005371/en/State-Industry-Candles-U.S.-2017-Edition-- .

If you can find a way to make your candles unique, you can position yourself above the rest of the candle makers! As an example, if you specialize in one-of-a-kind all-natural soy and beeswax candles designed with an element of wonderment and surprise that is unique to each candle, customers will start to recognize that candle as "your" candle line and "the line of candles they always buy."

To establish yourself as a quality candle brand, always use quality ingredients for your candles. Make sure the packaging is neat and attractive. It can be simple but needs to represent your company well and appeal to your target audience.

Packaging is an important marketing tool that can make or break your business.

If you're marketing candles to mature women, you'll probably want to skip the neon green labeling and packaging, but that packaging may be quite appropriate for marketing candles to pre-teen and teen girls.

4 EFFECTIVE MARKETING IDEAS

1. Always run one special where you offer discount on one particular type of candle each month, but never the same type of candles every month
2. Run BOGO (Buy One Get One Free) promotion every few months on select candles (usually the ones that are not selling fast)
3. Never try to be the low price leader (It is a slippery slope, don't try to reduce your price just to stay competitive)
4. Run various package promotion during holidays (I usually make baskets with few candles, one bottle of aromatherapy essential

oil, one soap and a candle holder all nicely wrapped)

Remember, when it comes to pricing or marketing ideas, there is no "one size fits all," not every idea works for everyone. Some strategies may work better for you than others and vice versa. So, it is a good idea to test each idea separately and document the results then analyze and see which one worked the best.

The candle business is a creative one. Be just as creative with your marketing and sales as you are with your candle creations and you will see success!

IN REVIEW AND CONCLUSION

Learn as much as you can about the craft of making candles. The more techniques you learn and the more you learn about the tools and supplies available for candle making, the more versatility you have for creating unique, highly-marketable candles.

Find your niche and stick with that niche until you become confident and may want to spread your wings and expand.

It's better to make a few quality styles and shapes of candles than to make several styles and shapes of lower quality candles. Make the candles that you want to be known for in the candle business. This will establish you as a professional.

Schedule and spend plenty of time marketing your candle business as well as keeping your inventory stocked.

When you are a small business, you must wear many hats, including the hat of the creative artist, business owner, bookkeeper, salesperson, marketer, and merchandiser.

Pay attention to the numbers and keep good records. Just because you love what you do, it doesn't mean that you shouldn't be making a profit and know where your business stands financially.

Creative types may not be great with numbers, but numbers are the essential point for your business. Keep good records or hire someone to keep them for you.

If your business flails as you learn, don't panic and close the business. Know that it's normal to flail a bit when you start a new business.

This is how you learn valuable lessons and work out all the glitches of your business. Give yourself plenty of time for the learning curve and keep going. You are on your way to a successful candle business!

LAST WORDS

I want to say THANK YOU for purchasing and reading this book. I really hope you got a lot out of it!

Can I ask you for a quick favor though?

If you enjoyed this book, I would really appreciate it if you could leave me a Review on Amazon.

I LOVE getting feedback from my wonderful readers, and reviews on Amazon really do make the difference. I read all of my reviews and would love to hear your thoughts.

Thank you so much!!

Rebecca Hall

P. S. You can go directly to the book on Amazon and leave your review. In the event, you need to get in touch with me, please feel free to email me at rolpublishing@gmail.com

APPENDIX – ARTICLES OF INCORPORATION

Here is a basic and standard articles of incorporation, please use this just as an example. When incorporating your own business it is important to seek legal advice.

There are many online sites where you can get articles like this done for less than $100, sites like leaglzoom.com, but my advice is do your own Google search and see who is offering a better deal as there are many reputable sites out there.

ARTICLES OF ORGANIZATION

OF

BOUTIQUE CANDLES LLC

The undersigned, acting as organizers of the Boutique Candles LLC under the Georgia Limited Liability Company Act, adopt the following Articles of Organization for said Limited Liability Company.

Article I

Name of the Company

The name of the limited liability company is Boutique Candles LLC (the "Company").

Article II

Period of Duration

The period of duration is ninety (90) years from the date of filing of these Articles of Organization with the Georgia Secretary of State, unless the Company is sooner dissolved.

Article III

Purpose of the Company

The Company is organized to engage in all legal and lawful purpose of producing and selling candles and candle related products.

Article IV

Registered Office and Agent

The Company's registered office is at address is 123 Main Street, Atlanta, Georgia, 30301; and the name and the address of the Company's initial registered agent is Jane Doe, 123 Main Street, Atlanta, Georgia, 30301.

Article V

Members of the Organization

There is one (1) member, all of which are identified in the Exhibit A attached hereto and a part hereof. The initial capital contribution agreed to be made by both members are also listed on Exhibit A. The members have not agreed to make any additional contributions, but may agree to do so in the future upon the terms and conditions as set forth in the Operating Agreement.

Article VI

Additional Members

The members, as identified in the Company's Operating Agreement, reserve the right to admit additional members and determine the Capital Contributions of such Members. Notwithstanding the foregoing, the additional Members may not become managing unless and until selected to such position as provided in Article VII of the Company's Operating Agreement.

Article VII

Contribution upon Withdrawal of Members

The members shall have the right to continue the company upon the death, retirement, resignation, expulsion, bankruptcy or dissolution of a member or occurrence of any event which terminates the continued membership of a member in the Company (collectively, "Withdrawal"), as long as there is at least One remaining member, and the remaining member agree to continue the Company by unanimous written consent within 90 days after the Withdrawal of a Member, as set forth in the Operating Agreement of the Company.

Article VIII

Manager

The name and business address of the initial manager is:

Jane Doe

Boutique Candles LLC

123 Main Street

Atlanta, Georgia, 30301

The manager may be removed and replaced by the Members as provided in the Operating Agreement.

IN WITNESS WHEREOF, the undersigned have caused these Articles of Organization to be executed this ……………. Day of ……………………….. 2012

_____

_____

       Boutique Candles LLC

DATE

AN ALABAMA CORPORATION

BY: Jane Doe

ITS: Managing Member

This instrument prepared by:

Jane Doe

123 Main Street

Atlanta, Georgia, 30301

EXHIBIT A

MEMBERS   INTIAL CONTRIBUTION
INTEREST

Jane Doe   Future Services Rendered
100%

APPENDIX –B BUSINESS PLAN

BOUTIQUE CANDLES LLC

BUSINESS PLAN

I. EXECUTIVE SUMMARY

Boutique candles LLC, (hereinafter "Business") is intended to be formed as a Georgia Limited Liability Company (LLC) located at 123 Main Street, Atlanta, Georgia 30301, poised for rapid growth in the Candle Making Industry. The Business seeks funding to take advantage of a window of opportunity for introducing a new Boutique Candles product, which has the potential to dominate the market.

Mission Statement. Boutique Candles LLC is a unique candle making company that produces high quality, all natural aromatic candles made from all natural beeswax and purer soy. At BCL our mission to prosper and thrive in the billion dollar candle industry as a leader of the most natural and aromatic candles maker in this industry.

Business Description. The Business is to be organized as a Limited Liability Company (LLC) formed and authorized under the laws of the State of Georgia, and will be led by Jane Doe, who will serve as CEO.

Jane a wife and a mother of four has been in the various craft related businesses for more than a decade. She love to explore essential oil, their core benefits and use for many years.

New Product. The Business has developed a Boutique Candles product which has the following specifications:

All natural Beeswax and Soy Candles

The Business has a window of opportunity to introduce its products and gain a significant piece of the market share.

Funding Request. The total funding request is for a $250.00 loan for a period of 7 years. The funding proceeds will be used as follows:

$15,000.00 for Marketing

This amount is earmarked for effectively marketing the products as described below in the Marketing Summary section of the Business Plan.

$10,000.00 for Staffing

This portion of funding is intended for hiring employees to produce the products and assist marketing and sales efforts.

$150,000.00 for Machineries, equipment and molds

To acquire new and efficient candle making machines and equipment

The Business is looking for long-term debt funding. Financial projections forecast a break-even point in less than 24 months after product introduction. Conservative estimates show at least a 37% return on the investment by the end of the financing period.

II. BUSINESS SUMMARY

The business is a start-up business, providing clients with Boutique Candles.

Industry Overview. The Candle Making Industry in the United States currently generates $3.5 billion in annual sales. Annual revenue for the regional market where the business is located is estimated at $5 million.

Seasonal Factors. The Business would only be influenced by the seasonal factors that affect our customers. Since the demand for our services crosses many different businesses and industries, seasonal fluctuations are expected to be limited to the typical down turn in the dull period months are not affected by the annual holiday schedules.

Position in the Industry. BCL has a unique position in the market as the only natural candle making company using pure and natural beeswax that are sourced from local firms along with pure organic Soy products that are also sourced locally. Our candles are made 100% locally with local raw material, unlike our other competitors.

Legal Issues. The promoters have secured the required patents and trademarks for the products and processes of the business in accordance with the statutory requirements.

Location. BCL has secured a 4700 SQF warehouse in the CBD district, where we plan to renovate and make leasehold improvement of around $50,000 to make it efficient and productive. The lease is secured for next 15 years at $7/SQF/Year.

III. MARKETING SUMMARY

Target Markets. The main target markets for the business include:

- Local and regional candle retailers, Bath body stores, Farmer's markets, Flea Market, and many home craft stores. Not to mention we will be launching a new online store using Wix.com

It is estimated that there are 500 potential customers within the Business defined trading area that are estimated to spend $1,000,000.00. To seek the most profitable market segments in the target markets overall, the Business will focus on the following areas within the target market:

- We anticipate the biggest growth will come from our online sales channels

Competition. Customer choice of services in this industry is based on Price and Quality, we have mastered a balance between the two and positioned our candles accordingly.

Other candle makers local and national but what makes us stand out is our commitment to use all natural locally sourced raw materials.

Services. The Business intends to provide exceptional, personalized service, which will be the crucial factor in building and protecting the Business's brand within the community. The Business intends to handle customer concerns and issues with a customer oriented focus with the intent of providing timely resolution and preventing the loss of customers.

IV. STRATEGY AND IMPLEMENTATION SUMMARY

Company Goals and Objectives. We plan to grow our business by another 30% in next 24 months from online sales.

The Business plans the following tactics as part of sales promotion:

- Develop a list of businesses in the neighborhood and send brochures by direct mail to the list.

- Advertising through press releases to industry publications and local newspapers.

- Internet marketing

- Direct sales

- Posting signage and flyers about the new business on bulletin boards in stores and public places.

In addition, the Business will also engage in the following marketing campaigns:

- We plan to set up booths at many local events with samples, we will also use PPC ads online.

V. FINANCIAL PLAN

The Funding Request in this Business Plan outlines the major start-up costs associated with this business. Other costs include repair and maintenance, sales and production expenses. Regular monthly expenses are estimated at $8,950.00 for paying the employee salaries and other regular business expenses. The Business is expected to generate $775,000.00 in the first year, and gross profit is expected to be $459,000.00.

APPENDIX – C SAMPLE INVOICE

Invoice

Date: August 01, 2016

Invoice No: 001

Boutique candles LLC

123 Main Street

Atlanta, Georgia 30301

Bill to:

Customer: **John Doe**

555 Court street

Atlanta, Georgia 30302

Description	Quantity	Unit Price	Total Price
Assorted Candles	1,000	$3	$3,000

Subtotal: $3,000

Discount: 5% Discount Total: $150

Tax Rate: 0%Sales Tax: $0.00

Shipping Charges: $0.00

Purchase Total: $2,850

Make all checks payable to Boutique Candles LLC. If you have any questions regarding this invoice, contact Jane Doe by phone at 123-123-1234 or via email at Janedoe@email.com. Interest may accrue on any balance that remains unpaid after 30 days.

Thank you for your business.

Printed in Great Britain
by Amazon